1

10-Minute Philosophy:

From Buddhism to Stoicism, Confucius and Aristotle - Bite-Sized Wisdom From Some of History's Greatest Thinkers

By Patrick King
Social Skills Coach
www.PatrickKingConsulting.com

Table of Contents

Chapter 1. What's Your Philosophy?

Philosophy is one of those words that function like a Rorschach test.

A Rorschach test is otherwise known as the *inkblot test*. Certain types of psychologists show their patients an ambiguous image that vaguely resembles an inkwell spilled onto a piece of paper to gain insight into the perspectives and interpretations of their patient. The thought is that patients will see in the ambiguous image whatever they *want* to see in it, and that is representative of how they see the world, their emotional state, and so on.

Two people looking at the same blurry splotch of ink can see two vastly different images, and it will have nothing to do with the image itself. And so it is with philosophy.

I bring this up because philosophy isn't always viewed with positivity or even interest. If you think of philosophy as time-wasting thumb-twiddling, then that is undoubtedly what you will get out of it. You'll just hear a multitude of empty platitudes and wonder what the point of it all even is. This skeptical approach is fairly common and at times understandable. After all, what problems are being solved simply by *thinking and pontificating* about them? Indeed, if I'm hungry or in need of shelter right now, it's difficult to see the value that philosophy can add to someone's life.

What *tangible* benefit is there to figuring out the purpose of our lives?

Tangible? Zero. But philosophy was never about that. If you're looking for a field of study to enrich your immediate surroundings, I might suggest that you pick up an engineering or finance book. Philosophy has always been about enriching your thoughts for greater happiness and fulfillment—an immeasurable quantity, but perhaps the greatest purpose of all.

Admittedly, this was a mindset I also used to possess. If you were to create a hierarchy in society, especially in more ancient and brutal times, surely a philosopher would rank far lower than the average hunter, carpenter, or fisherman—at least in terms of pure utility. What was the role of a philosopher in a society beyond their teaching duties?

But consider how our ancestors were able to figure out calculus, discern the relative size of the earth, and map out constellations. Eventually, when food and shelter weren't immediate concerns, people were able to just sit and *think about things*, and this freedom of time is how humans were able to advance. Philosophers became repositories of knowledge and discourse.

They became explorers, discoverers, and scientists. It is certainly no coincidence that when we look back at the lives of the most famous philosophers in history, they invariably were also scientists, teachers, and even mathematicians.

The human need for understanding (some might say a sense of control) of their surroundings is insatiable, and it's only natural that it would eventually spill over from practical concerns such as agriculture and calculus into topics such as purpose, ethics, morality, meaning, knowledge, and how to live. To evoke Maslow's hierarchy of needs, once our physical and then emotional needs are satisfied, we will inevitably turn our attention to learning, wisdom, exploration, and fulfillment.

The word "philosophy" comes from the Greek phrase meaning "love of wisdom." And who doesn't want more wisdom? Philosophers began with an intense curiosity about the mysterious world around them and sought out answers in the only way they could.

They didn't have the benefit of science or technology to find answers, so they had to start from ground zero and use thinking, reasoning, and critical analysis to gain truth and knowledge. How might you determine why men and women are different or why the sun rises in the morning? The only place you can start is by thinking and pondering, making observations, and then challenging everything you thought you knew. This is perhaps why philosophy can appear circular and redundant, constantly asking *Why do you know what you think you know*? That's all they had, and you'll get a full dose of that approach when you read later on about Rene Descartes.

They grappled with questions that we still can't prove or definitively answer even with today's technological advances. But this didn't deter them.

What is life? What is right and wrong? What is our purpose? How should we live our lives? What is real and what is not?

Philosophy seeks to answer these questions, and by and large, different schools of philosophy sprang out of different answers and approaches. We're nowhere closer to objective answers to any of those questions some two millennia later, but many perspectives have been created, each with the possibility of increasing your happiness and fulfillment—your true benefit from learning philosophy.

This will ultimately be the purpose of this book: exploring a set of approaches to fulfillment and finding one that helps you find your personal version of it. You might find that none of the approaches resonate except one. In that case, feel free to discard what you don't like. You might find that each of them resonates in their own way, and in that case, cobble together a Frankenstein version of your approach to happiness, taking bits and pieces from everything.

But as you will see from the following thought experiment, it's not so easy as simply steering your ship toward a destination.

The Trolley Dilemma

One of the most famous philosophical questions comes in the form of the *trolley dilemma*, and it is a question of ethics and morality. You can think of this problem as determining what is moral and what is not, for yourself and others. In doing so, you might find that your idea of morality directly conflicts with that of others.

It was originally developed as a thought experiment by Philippa Foot in 1967 and adapted by Judith Thomson afterward, and the nature of any dilemma is that it produces different answers that demand to be examined. There is fertile ground for disagreement and exploration of different interpretations. Each different answer underlies a different set of values and formative life experiences.

Imagine you are standing beside some trolley tracks. You see a runaway trolley screaming down the tracks toward five workers who are facing away from it and don't hear it coming. Even if they miraculously become aware of their imminent mortality, they are still doomed to their deaths.

You are an innocent bystander, and you fortunately have some knowledge of how trolley tracks work. You see a lever that is connected to the tracks within touching distance, and you realize that if you were to pull the lever, the trolley would be diverted down a second set of tracks and the five workers would be saved.

However—and this is where the dilemma comes in—you would be diverting the trolley down a track that would kill one worker. So would you pull the lever and save five people at the expense of one? Would you even act? Could you think in a utilitarian way and reason to yourself that you are actually saving four lives? And would any of those types of thinking affect the amount of guilt you might feel?

What about if you didn't move a muscle—would you be morally wrong for complete inaction? What if you didn't want to be responsible for making any decision at all? What if you believed in fatalism and the matter being out of your hands? What if you thought that one life was equal to four lives in the grand scheme of things, so why bother?

There is no wrong answer.

The trolley itself becomes a substitute for people and forces you to think through the consequences and whether the rightness or wrongness of an action is determined solely by the outcome or by the intentions. In studies and surveys, it turns out most people would pull the lever and divert the trolley to kill one person while sparing five. It seems that instinctually we are mostly utilitarians at heart and will do what is best for the greatest number of people.

But does that mean we would sacrifice ourselves in order to let a boatful of children live? What if the five workers were all convicted murderers and the single worker was on par with Mother Teresa's impact? What if they were five elderly people with raging cancer? The permutations of what these choices can mean and what they say about us are endless. There are no correct or incorrect answers when you are seeking to gain wisdom and knowledge—even an answer that says "I would try to make sure all six people are killed" is not incorrect and provides a valid perspective.

We all inherently want to do good, for ourselves and others—or do we?

If this is starting to sound confusing, welcome to your quick introduction to philosophical thinking. The trolley dilemma is merely an example of the type of information and knowledge we can gain from simple pondering and thinking; it's far from a useless pursuit, as these types of considerations influence law, policy, and decisions on both conscious and subconscious levels. In this case, you are forced to explore what it means to be ethical and moral. You will see that there is no such thing as a simple answer inside of a vacuum.

Philosophical thinking may not provide tangible benefits in itself, but the process you use to get there certainly will.

Philosophy Is About Thinking

What kind of approach do you need in order to have any hope of making sense of the trolley dilemma? For starters, you need a sense of analysis, logic, organization, and the overall ability to think in terms of consequences and implications. When you go down one thread of thought, what are the considerations that arise from it, why do they exist, and what do they lead to? If that leads to a dead end, then you need to be able to backtrack and explore other perspectives with thoroughness.

Philosophy requires the unfiltered skill of critical thinking and analysis. It's something that we constantly pay lip service to but don't really delve into the meaning of.

Unfortunately this does take considerable effort, as it runs counter to how our brains are wired.

Philosophy is about the pursuit of thinking, and it teaches analysis of arguments, logical constructions, and critical reasoning. It teaches cognitive biases and logical fallacies, as well as a sense of discovery because, as you can see, no one answer is ever enough. You must always go deeper; there is always a next level down to explore. Your view is always limited and biased; how can you take on a different perspective? While it may sound tedious, for the lover of wisdom, it's a good thing. You'll challenge your own point of view and understand why others have merit.

For instance, in the trolley dilemma, it's about solving a problem with no real answer. With philosophy, you gain creative problem-solving skills. You learn to organize and classify information in a multitude of ways, all useful to a particular purpose. You'll learn how to construct an argument and identify points that say what they are representing, as well as those that are basically deceptions.

Perhaps the greatest and most adaptable skill you gain from philosophy is the ability to function and even thrive in the ambiguous. This is something else that we are wired against—we typically want certainty, especially in the face of a question or problem. But in philosophy, there are no true answers, only multiple valid perspectives. Where does that leave you?

Needing to cultivate a set of techniques to question and understand deeper—these are the wandering and circuitous thoughts that appear to lead to nowhere to the casual observer but in reality are drilling down deep into knowledge and wisdom. With this ability comes a certain open-mindedness of what each different perspective entails. That's something that no one is born with and that we must gain through practice.

So if you are skeptical about why you might want to pick this book up or read on, there are very real benefits to learning philosophy—just not if you're hungry or in need of a place to sleep in the rain. Life is not typically certain or concrete, so abstract thinking will assist you considerably.

Yet this still pales in comparison to the value of finding your life philosophy, a personalized path to fulfillment and happiness based on some of history's greatest thinkers.

What's Your Life Philosophy?

Philosophy gives you hard skills, some might even say *marketable* and *employable* skills—even if a degree in philosophy is not known as such.

But philosophy arguably gives you the most important thing you can have as a person— clarity on your own views, values, and perspectives. And it's only through understanding those aspects that you can understand how to create the best life for yourself.

How did you answer the trolley dilemma? Would you have pulled that lever? What went through your head as you made your decision?

That's who you are at the current moment, for better or worse. That's where you stand on the spectrum of morality and ethics. It may just be a simple yes or no on pulling the lever, but it speaks to so much more of how you view the world and your place in it. Your actions stem from your values and morals, and it behooves you to understand why you do the things you do.

Philosophy imparts self-understanding, one of the rarest qualities in the world. You understand what appeals to you and what you simply couldn't care less about. From self-understanding, you can build the life you want. Imagine if a doctor were to prescribe a course of antibiotics based on only the symptoms and not the causes of an illness. That's what we are dealing with if we lack self-understanding.

This is what I would refer to as a *life philosophy*—a code of behavior and mindsets that you seek to live your life by to optimize your happiness. They are rules you set for yourself to fulfill your values on a daily basis. The simplest example is someone who endlessly pursues money to the detriment of their relationships. Clearly their philosophy is oriented on wealth, and they gain self-worth from it—even if they don't know it or want to admit it. If they know it, they can orient themselves toward what fulfills them and avoid that which does not. It's all we are really looking for in life.

Everyone has a life philosophy, but most don't know they do, and even fewer are able to describe it. If you were to ask someone, it would most likely be someone else's philosophy parroted back at you. This is simply because most of us don't know who we are or what we want from life. We are directionless, or we simply float through the path of least resistance and pain.

A life philosophy helps you avoid all that by clarifying what is and is not important. That is the biggest benefit of the study of philosophy, and indeed this book seeks to provide the life philosophies of some pretty sharp thinkers to emulate or disregard. What was Aristotle's take on happiness and fulfillment, and how does that compare to Marcus Aurelius's or Confucius's? Does the life philosophy of stoicism align with your values more, or do you prefer the principles of Taoism? What texts shed light on what's important to you, what you want to avoid, and what you want to emulate? Surely we can learn from these titans of thought.

Living without a life philosophy is like sailing a boat without a map, engine, or even end destination in mind. You're probably seeking contentment and happiness, but you don't know where it is. You don't know what direction you're headed in, and even if you knew, you would have no way to change course. You simply drift according to life's external forces on you. You might come to the frightening realization that you've spent your life drifting toward things you don't care about. You haven't chosen your own path; you've just acted as a vessel for the people and context surrounding you.

Learn about yourself, discover what is important, take responsibility for your own fulfillment, and directly pursue your own definition of happiness. Every small daily action acts to put us either further or closer to the correct course.

While an educational tour through some of history's greatest beliefs, *10-Minute Philosophy* is ultimately about better and happier living. It would be foolish if we didn't look into the past and borrow from ancient people's wisdom and apply it to our own modern lives. Each of the philosophies in this book has undergone thousands of years of scrutiny and has emerged intact. If you take away our modern trappings—electricity, Internet, and jet planes—not much has changed about us. Humans are still perpetually in search of happiness and fulfillment.

A final note before we start: this is not meant to be an in-depth primer on multiple sets of religions, philosophies, and belief systems. It is an introduction (10 minutes, so to speak) of what these philosophies espouse and how you might be able to fit them into your life for a boost of happiness and fulfillment. Of course, ancient beliefs cannot be distilled, but all it takes is a single thought or shift of mindset to dramatically alter your life. Think of it as a shot glass of instant wisdom for your review. Not everything is covered in grinding detail, and concepts have been left out purposefully for clarity's sake. We have one goal here—find a helpful path to happiness.

Takeaways:

- Philosophy means different things to different people, so I would like to present what it means to me. It's about self-understanding and then taking and stealing from some of history's greatest thinkers to form the basis of what makes you happy. It's only when you understand yourself that you can move forward in a way that is more likely to lead to your happiness. In other words, clearer thinking leads to self-understanding, which leads to your life philosophy emerging. Formulating your own life philosophy is key to the life you want, and it influences all of your daily actions, big and small.

- The trolley dilemma is a demonstration of the other major benefit of delving into philosophical thought. You learn how to think. You learn how to argue, debate, and reason. You learn how a seemingly innocent or simple question can have wide-ranging implications and consequences. You can learn to thrive in the ungrounded, abstract, and ambiguous. And when you direct this thinking toward deeper questions that philosophy presents, you can begin to understand yourself more than ever before.

- Philosophy won't directly feed your family or put a roof over your head, but indirectly, it leads to all that and more.

Chapter 2. Aristotle, Living Virtuously, and the Golden Mean

One of the first life philosophies we delve into is also one of the oldest and comes from a cluster of philosophical thought between two to three millennia ago. This particular life philosophy comes from Aristotle, of course known as one of Ancient Greece's most famous thinkers along with Socrates and Plato. You've probably seen pictures of his marble bust, even if you didn't know it was him.

Aristotle was the founder of the *Lyceum*, the first scientific institute in the ancient world in Athens, Greece. Along with his teacher and mentor, Plato, he originated numerous ideas about logic, science, and simply how to live. (By the way, Plato's teacher was Socrates.) They all lived and pontificated in Athens, which added to the reputation of the city as the birthplace of philosophical thought.

Aristotle was born in 384 BC in the Greek town of Stagiros, and it was said that his interest in science was inspired by his father, Nicomachus, who was a physician. At the age of 17, he traveled to Athens and studied under Plato at his renowned Academy, the preeminent school for philosophers and thinkers.

From there, he traveled to the court of Philip of Macedon and became childhood tutor to Alexander the Great, who you have probably heard of.

He accomplished a great many things, but what concerns us in this book is his perspective on fulfillment—better living and happiness. In fact, the achievement of fulfillment is what Aristotle felt was the true goal of every human. He felt that all human activities were done in order to attain some measure of fulfillment; if you weren't attaining fulfillment, then you were not acting in accord with his principles.

Fulfillment was known to him and ancient Greeks as *eudaemonia*, which is an important concept to first explore.

Eudaemonia

Eudaemonia is an Ancient Greek word that most closely resembles our modern conception of fulfillment. Obviously, it's what we should orient our lives toward, right?

When we try to articulate the purpose of our lives, we most commonly invoke the word fulfillment. We tell ourselves and others that the ultimate purpose of our jobs, our relationships, and the conduct of our day-to-day lives is the pursuit of fulfillment. It's an overarching feeling of contentment and satisfaction. However, the Ancient Greeks distinguished eudaemonia from *happiness*.

The difference between the two is *pain*. It is possible to be fulfilled via eudaemonia while suffering physical or mental pain, yet it is not possible to be happy while suffering pain. Happiness is a more temporary emotional state—it can be as powerful as a volcano yet vanish within an instant. Fulfillment is a long-term state of being that springs from living to our values and consciously choosing our lives. Eudaemonia operates as background music in our minds during hardships and tells us that everything will be just fine and remain in order. It's the feeling that despite temporary setbacks or obstacles, your life is still exactly what you want it to be.

If eudaemonia is the goal over happiness, then what is the best and most dependable way to eudaemonia?

No, it's not necessarily *seizing the day* (*carpe diem*) or satisfying your every whim and desire (hedonism). Neither is it achieving nirvana through deprivation (Buddhism) or accepting fate for what it is (Stoicism). Socrates held the belief that embodying traits such as courage, self-regulation, wisdom, and justice were the key to achieving eudaemonia. His prize pupil Plato felt that control over emotions and impulses and remaining rational at all times would lead one to eudaemonia.

Of course, Aristotle differed from all of the above.

In his view, eudaemonia was achieved by living virtuously, and one lives virtuously by adhering to traits of the Golden Mean. If you live your life with virtue, everything will be what you want it to be. As you can ascertain from the name, virtue (and thus a fulfilling life) is a result of moderating and regulating a select few desires and drives.

At its root, this is not such a foreign concept. We see such prescriptions from all types of religions—the Ten Commandments, for instance, which exist both in Christianity and Islam. But it's that tricky part about balance being the key that is a lesser-taken path to fulfillment.

Can we indulge in positive traits too much, to the point where it is detrimental? This is like asking if too much ice cream will be bad for you. Of course, there is always a tradeoff, and Aristotle clearly articulates the extremes that we must avoid to be virtuous and achieve eudaemonia.

The Golden Mean

From the name, you can already guess at what it's about. If not, it can be renamed Aristotle's "Goldilocks Principles," and the meaning would remain clear and nearly intact.

The Golden Mean is about seeking the middle, moderation, and not being an outlier as it pertains to specific traits. According to Aristotle, this was the path to a life full of virtue (and thus eudaemonia), and he articulated this concept in his book *Nicomachean Ethics*. The origin of the book's title is unknown, but knowing that his father was named Nicomachus, it wouldn't be a stretch to assume that it was to pay homage to his father's teachings and beliefs. *Nicomachean Ethics* was written around 340 BC and the work itself is actually a series of lectures that was later pieced together and published as a complete work.

As Aristotle defines it, the Golden Mean is the exact middle point between two extremes, where one side verges on excess and the other side verges on deficiency. Aristotle cleverly positioned himself between a rock and a hard place, where the only solution was to avoid both.

Both extremes are vices, and thus the only virtuous path is between the two of them. Therefore, choosing the medium route every time will slowly and surely lead you to eudaemonia. This results in a healthy balance of quelling desires (no excesses) and forcing you out of your comfort zone (no deficiencies).

One should not be too brave or too cowardly, as the brave is foolhardy and the cowardly is fearful. One should not be too emotional, but neither should he be too inexpressive. He should not be too light-hearted but also not too serious and stoic. He should be open-minded yet not be too easily swayed, as the open-minded has no conviction and the not easily swayed can be stubborn to the point of ignorance. Don't be lazy, but don't be overly consumed by your pursuits as to fall ill or neglect other areas of your life.

Don't eat too much, but don't starve yourself. You get the idea. Aristotle has a few underlying beliefs that resulted in his formulation of the Golden Mean.

First, the physically and medically healthy person is balanced. They have an equilibrium within them. For instance, a man or woman's temperature can't stray too high or low, and the human body can't eat too much or too little. Here, moderation can literally be the difference between life and death. One's body cannot and should not go to extremes, and thus the character should not—equilibrium should be sought in terms of virtues and traits.

Second, each person's mean/middle point is relative and unique. Fulfillment, of course, cannot be objective because different pursuits make different people happy. People have different tolerances and proclivities that must be taken into account. Someone who is two meters tall must have a different type of diet than someone who is only 1.5 meters tall—both should eat at a level of moderation, but this level will be wildly different in proportion. One who seeks fulfillment through food must find the mean between being a glutton and starving. Each person's definition of excess and deficiency is their own. Knowing exactly what is appropriate in a given situation is difficult.

Third, the Golden Mean is self-perpetuating. Remember that virtue lies between two extremes. Thus, if you draw too near to either extreme, you will start to receive social backlash. If you stay close to the mean, you will receive praise from others and fulfillment from yourself. You will be naturally reinforced to continue seeking moderated behavior based on this praise and positivity. What feels good will be what we strive to do.

Nearly everything about the Golden Mean lends itself to a life philosophy. You may not necessarily agree that you should avoid excess, but at the very least, we can all agree that we must avoid deficiencies. But then again, can't we categorize excesses as deficiencies relative to something else?

In the end, too much of anything has its drawbacks. Too much of a good thing ends up being a bad thing, and bad things, well, become even worse things. We can get closer to the specifics of Aristotle's recommended way of living when we delve into the specific deficiencies and excesses he wrote about.

Virtue Versus Vices

Aristotle possessed the belief that virtue (and thus eudaemonia) would spring from moderation of 11 specific traits, which again are right at the midpoint between excess and deficiency. The first trait we will cover is courage, and courage is the midpoint between reckless action (excess) and cowardice (deficiency). Too much courage and you will leap without thinking; too little courage and you will make only fear-based decisions.

Below is a handy diagram with all the vices and virtues neatly displayed to gain a sense of context before diving into each individual scale.

Aristotle's Golden Mean — Philosophy

Sphere of action or feeling	Excess	Mean	Deficiency
Fear and confidence	Rashness *thrasutes*	Courage *andreia*	Cowardice *deilia*
Pleasure and pain	Licentiousness *akolasia*	Temperance *sophrosune*	Insensibility *anaisthesia*
Getting and spending (minor)	Prodigality *asotia*	Liberality *eleutheriotes*	Illiberality / Meanness *aneleutheria*
Getting and spending (major)	Vulgarity *apeirokalia, banausia*	Magnificence *megaloprepeia*	Pettiness *mikroprepeia*
Honor and dishonor (major)	Vanity *chaunotes*	Magnanimity *megalopsuchia*	Pusillanimity *mikropsuchia*
Honor and dishonor (minor)	Ambition *philotimia*	Proper ambition	Unambitiousness *aphilotimia*
Anger	Irascibility *orgilotes*	Patience *praotes*	Lack of spirit *aorgesia*
Self-expression	Boastfulness *alazoneia*	Truthfulness *aletheia*	Understatement *eironeia*
Conversation	Buffoonery *bomolochia*	Wittiness *eutrapelia*	Boorishness *agroikia*
Social conduct	Obsequiousness *areskeia* / Flattery *kolakeia*	Friendliness *philia (?)*	Cantankerousness *duskolia /duseris*
Shame	Shyness *kataplexis*	Modesty *aidos*	Shamelessness *anaischuntia*
Indignation	Envy *phthonos*	Righteous indignation *nemesis*	Malicious enjoyment *epichairekakia*

Courtesy of BCresources.net

But Aristotle places another requirement around his articulated virtues. For Aristotle, virtue "is a habit disposed toward action by deliberate choice, being at the mean relative to us, and defined by reason as a prudent man would define it."

This means virtue is only achieved through deliberately and intentionally choosing the Golden Mean because it is the noble and correct thing to do. Unlike other philosophies where only the actions are judged, Aristotle judges both intent and action. If you act within the Golden Mean by accident, unintentionally, or because it was your only choice, then you will not attain fulfillment.

There is no accidental virtue, and the outcome is not the only important thing in achieving eudaemonia. This sounds exhausting, but this parallels our emotions in real life. Simply put, are you virtuous when you are commanded to clean the house, even if it is the right and fair thing to do? No, and the fact that you are upset by this command makes it clear that you are knowingly shirking your responsibilities—and not being virtuous.

In the end, it becomes a tall task, but whoever said the path to fulfillment was supposed to be easy?

Virtue #1: Courage. This is the mean between rashness and cowardice. Courage is when you face your fears because it is the right thing to do. A courageous person will make sure their actions are measured and intelligent but not be ruled by fear. There is a healthy zone of action for confronting fears (of public speaking, for instance) but also realizing your limitations and reality (not fighting an attacking bear).

Virtue #2: Temperance. This is the mean between physical pain and pleasure. You can imagine how this is a strong drive that must be regulated. A temperate person will understand that pleasure is not perpetual and pain is a necessary part of life. They will simply do the noble and correct action instead of avoiding pain or seeking pleasure. This notion of temperance is a corollary of mental toughness and self-discipline. Pain is often the only path there is.

Virtue #3: Generosity. Generosity toward others is the mean between stinginess and wastefulness. This virtue is about the habit of giving and charity, where stinginess is not giving at all and wastefulness is giving too much. A generous person will give what they can because they possess empathy for others. However, they will not give so much, as generosity requires the giver to be able to take care of themselves first.

Virtue #4: Munificence. This virtue is about how you utilize your resources with regards to yourself, and it is the mean between meanness (deficiency) and ostentatiousness (excess). We can see this in the modern day as the difference between *want* and *need*. We want many things, but we need far fewer. Don't allow yourself to live like a pauper, but living like a king is unnecessary and gaudy. The munificent man seeks comfort and security, not luxury and entitlement. Don't avoid spending for what matters, and don't overspend for what doesn't.

Virtue #5: Magnanimity. This virtue is the mean between arrogance/vanity and insecurity. It is the difference between a lack of self-worth and an inflated sense of ego. Everyone has accolades and can claim honor or credit. But this doesn't mean that you should always do this. To focus on honors, even if you deserve them, is to be overly concerned with recognition and how you are viewed by others. To overly ignore them, however, is to shrink out of fear and hesitation. The magnanimous person recognizes their worth and accurately represents themselves.

Virtue #6. Seeking honor. This is somewhat related to the previous virtue of magnanimity. There, virtue was found by only accurately seeking recognition. Here, virtue is found by how much ambition you have toward actions worthy of recognition. In other words, you should have high ambition, but not so much that it consumes the rest of your life. On the other hand, you can't have too little ambition such that you are left without purpose.

Virtue #7: Good temper. The virtue of good temper is apparent. It sits between excessive bitterness/volatility and emotional apathy. Someone with a good temper can regulate their emotions but still become angry at the right people, at the right time, for the right actions, and for the right length of time. Extreme emotions are an inescapable part of life, but you cannot let them control you, nor can you ignore them. Be levelheaded.

Virtue #8: Friendliness. This virtue more or less measures how pleasant you are as company. It sits between sycophantism/flattery and antisocial/argumentative tendencies. A friendly person is open and communicative yet not to the point of catering or patronizing. At the other end, they can resist conflict for conflict's sake. In the end, a virtuously friendly person knows when to compliment but also when to assert and draw boundaries.

Virtues #9: Truthfulness. This is the mean between boastfulness and self-depreciation. Truthfulness has to do with how honest you are regarding your own abilities. You don't need to shrink yourself for others, but neither should you seek to puff yourself up for them. The mean point here shows comfort and security in your identity and accomplishments. Be honest and straightforward.

Virtue #10: Wit. A wit is a healthy sense of humor with the ability to understand and know when humor is appropriate or not. This is the mean between buffoonery (excess) and being obtuse and boorish (deficiency). A witty person recognizes that interactions are fueled by humor and amusement. Too much wit and you become a dancing jester; too little wit and you become a negative presence.

Virtue #11: Justice. Interestingly, justice is the mean between an excess of unfairness and a deficiency of unfairness. Too much justice is unfair because it robs you of empathy, and too little justice is unfair

43

because then there is no sense of equality of treatment. Typically, we rely on laws and customs to deliver justice, but they are not always applicable or fair themselves. Someone interested in justice will dole out appropriate consequences, but keep in mind the ever-present human element for why events have transpired.

You might have assumed that he would have included traits such as kindness, respect, self-discipline, or spirituality or aspects that we can generally trace back to the aforementioned Ten Commandments. In the end, Aristotle presents a selection of 11 virtues for which the selection process is unclear, but he clearly struck a societal chord from his knowledge and experiences.

To clarify, these are Aristotle's 11 *moral* virtues. He goes on in *Nicomachean Ethics* to describe five *intellectual* virtues. The intellectual virtues are less about prescribing a life philosophy and more about how to think more effectively. Those are worthy pursuits as well, but they don't impact our general fulfillment as directly.

According to Aristotle, the intellectual virtues include scientific knowledge (*episteme*), artistic or technical knowledge (*techne*), intuitive reason (*nous*), practical wisdom (*phronesis*), and philosophic wisdom (*sophia*). Just for posterity's sake, a brief description of them follows:

1. Scientific knowledge allows you to understand cause and effect and draw conclusions from real facts and principles.
2. Artistic knowledge allows the creation of things that previously only existed in someone's imagination.
3. Intuitive reasoning is what we today might call "street smarts" and provides insight into how the world works, which can supplement scientific and artistic knowledge.
4. Practical wisdom is what intuitive reasoning becomes after experience and practice. It allows you to make smart choices for decisions.
5. Philosophic wisdom can be said to be the ultimate level of intellectual virtue, as it removes oneself from the physical

world and examines issues that are arguably more significant.

Back to the Golden Mean. For most people, mere awareness is not enough to make them act virtuously. Consequently, laws are necessary to keep people in check. This goes against intention and action needing to match, but at least it's a starting point to keep society in order.

What we can keep in mind are a few powerful lessons from Aristotle. Extremes are dangerous because they trap us into singular modes of thinking, and this can blind us. Moderation is necessary because it allows us to see the error of our ways. Action without intention is sometimes worthless because there is no accidental virtue.

And fulfillment and eudaemonia? It's a process, not a destination. Intentionally follow the Golden Mean and you'll get there as a byproduct.

Friendship

Though most of the discussion involving
Nicomachean Ethics rightfully revolves
around the moral virtues that Aristotle
espoused, he later goes on to describe
another aspect he feels is key to living well.

Unlike a set of strict moral virtues, this is
something that we have probably given
thought to before. He is a large proponent
for how friendships enrich our lives and
how they bring fulfillment and happiness.
But true to form, Aristotle complicates
things by first defining friendship and the
particular types of friendship that best lead
to fulfillment.

What is *our* definition of friendship? The
offhand definition would be something
involving shared positive experiences,
companionship, and emotional intimacy. It's
not far off from Aristotle's definition, which
invokes goodwill, love, and shared values—
and, of course, virtue.

He articulates three types of friendships, one of which is to be pursued over the other two. The first two types of friendships are less intentional and more about temporary companionship—remember what Aristotle said about intentionality being a required element of virtue?

The first type of friendship is one of *utility*. In this type of friendship, the two parties are not seeking affection or even companionship; they spend time together more so because each party receives a benefit in exchange. It's a friendship borne out of convenience, proximity, or even loneliness.

It's not permanent in nature, and whenever the benefit ends, so does the reason that brought the people together. Aristotle observed this to be more common in older folks, though my personal observation is that it is occurring more in younger folks, such as work and school friends. You are in close proximity with them, but once someone is no longer there, you don't feel any type of emptiness or longing toward them. You may enjoy the time you spend together, but once the situation changes, so does the nature of your connection.

The second type of friendship is based on pleasure. Not of the carnal type (though it can be), but it's the kind of friendship frequently seen among college friends or people who participate on the same sports team.

The reason these friendships are categorized as pleasure-based is because they are made during a pleasurable experience. The source and linchpin of the friendship is a positive emotional experience; the parties can enjoy it together, as they will amplify each other's emotions. But these friendships will end as soon as either tastes or preferences change. For instance, what if one of these friends were to switch sports team allegiances?

Most of the friendships that many of us have fall into one or both of these two categories, and while Aristotle didn't necessarily see them as things to be avoided, he did feel that their depth limited their quality. It can't be a negative thing to have many acquaintances and people you can talk and relate with. It's necessary, even, sometimes, to be able to take comfort in the anonymity of relative strangers. But Aristotle astutely observed that these two friendships wouldn't lead to fulfillment.

Aristotle's most fulfilling form of friendship is based on a mutual appreciation of the *virtues* that the other party values. Each party wants to be close and emotionally intimate with the other because they want to be close to those traits and virtues. Aristotle explains here:

> The perfect form of friendship is that between the good, and those who resemble each other in virtue. For these friends wish each alike the other's good in respect of their goodness, and they are good in themselves, but it is those who wish the good of their friends for their friends' sake who are friends in the fullest sense since they love each

other for themselves and not accidentally.

Hence the friendship of these lasts as long as they continue to be good, and virtue is a permanent quality. And each is good relatively to his friend as well as absolutely, since the good are both good absolutely and profitable to each other. And each is pleasant in both ways also, since good men are pleasant both absolutely and to each other; for everyone is pleased by his own actions, and therefore by actions that resemble his own, and the actions of all good men are the same or similar.

These friendships often last quite long because they are self-perpetuating and based on things that are more permanent. Utility and pleasure can change at the drop of a hat, but a person's virtues and character likely will not. Such virtuous friendships create mutual growth and are uplifting forces in your life. They take time and trust to cultivate but produce the most benefit and fulfillment.

It's as simple as the following statement: when you respect someone, you enjoy being around them and allow yourself to learn from them. In that way, utility is also created—and occasionally pleasure as well. But it's the matching and mutually admired values that form the bedrock of lasting friendships that lead to eudaemonia.

Aristotle found friendship to be a glue that holds cities and societies together. In this belief also contains the message that the right relationships are the key to our greatest *external* sources of happiness—the rest is up to us by adhering to chasing virtue and the Golden Mean.

Takeaways:

- We can consider this chapter to be the life philosophy of Aristotle with regards to seeking happiness and fulfillment or, in his term, eudaemonia. It was all about virtue for him. Eudaemonia sprung from living a virtuous life, and virtue was attained by adhering to the Golden Mean.

- The Golden Mean is a set of 11 traits to exemplify and ensure that you are not using them to excess or deficiency. In other words, it's just as you would assume from the title: a life of moderation and even keel. Yes, too much of a good thing ends up being a bad thing; there are always tradeoffs. When you live within these 11 traits, you will automatically be living the life that makes you fulfilled, no matter the outcomes or circumstances. Of note, you must intentionally (and not accidentally) be embodying these traits to be virtuous.
- The Golden Mean is a means of finding eudaemonia internally from your own actions. Aristotle also addressed how to externally find fulfillment—through the right types of friendships. He articulated three types: pleasure-based, utility-based, and virtue-based. Of course, he's all about virtues again here and the mutual growth and respect they encourage.

Chapter 3. Buddhism and the Elimination of Attachment

We now come to the first of our eastern life philosophies, and unlike the other two to follow, there are still a significant number of Buddhist practitioners in the modern age.

Buddhism began in India in the sixth century BC as a branch of Hinduism. But most of the origin story of Buddhism focuses on the founder, Siddhartha Gautama. In fact, his story would become one of the archetypes for various religious figures for centuries to come. His journey culminated in Gautama eventually assuming the role of the eponymous

Buddha that we refer to, even though Buddhism isn't necessarily about deity worship.

There are various versions with slight changes in details here and there, but the generally accepted life story of Siddhartha Gautama is that he was a rich prince who lived in luxury. He lived a life so sheltered that various accounts mention that he never even stepped outside the walls of his palace until he was in his late 20s, after he had married and fathered a child.

When he did, what he saw shocked him. He saw poverty, old age, and sickness. He saw death and unhappiness in all its forms. He was so moved by what he saw that the very next day he left his palace and family to dedicate his life to ridding the world of such suffering. He believed that his method to solve this problem was through understanding the root of unhappiness and how people could find fulfillment even with such drastic conditions around them.

He emulated those conditions by fasting, refusing food and water, and almost dying of starvation. He underwent extreme physical deprivation in his attempt to gain perspective. But whatever he tried, Siddhartha could not reach the level of satisfaction he sought, until one day when a young girl offered him a bowl of rice. As he accepted it, he suddenly realized that physical suffering was not the means to achieve inner liberation and that living under harsh physical constraints was not helping him achieve spiritual release.

From then on, Siddhartha encouraged people to follow a path of balance instead of one characterized by extremism. He called this path the Middle Way. That night, Siddhartha sat under a Bodhi tree, vowing to not get up until the truths he sought came to him, and he meditated until the sun came up the next day. He remained there for seven weeks, ruminating on how to achieve the Middle Way. This Middle Way is a psychological-philosophical insight into the cause and cure of suffering and evil. And soon a picture began to form in his mind of all that occurred in the universe, and Siddhartha finally saw the answer to the questions of suffering that he had been seeking for so many years.

He finally reached what we might deem the path to enlightenment, and for our purposes, it takes three sequential forms: the Three Marks of Existence, the Four Noble Truths, and the Eightfold Path. In that moment of pure enlightenment, Siddhartha Gautama became the Buddha ("he who is awake/enlightened").

For the remainder of his 80 years, Buddha traveled, preaching the Dharma (the name given to the teachings of the Buddha) in an effort to lead others to and along the path of enlightenment.

As far as life philosophies go, Buddhism is one of the more instructive and direct ones on reaching fulfillment—or enlightenment, as Buddha himself reached. A clear premise and path are set out, starting with the Three Marks of Existence.

The Reality: The Three Marks of Existence

When we talk about Buddhism, we must start from his view of the world—the universal drives and tendencies of every living thing. They are simply a part of the fabric of our lives. Only from there can we construct a path to deal with them.

He called these aspects the Three Marks of Existence, and this is another aspect in which Buddha provides the underlying symptoms and causes for what makes us unfulfilled and lean away from nirvana. It is important to understand these marks, as they inform the Four Noble Truths, which are a direct statement of the obstacles we face, subsequently the Eightfold Path to enlightenment and happiness.

The Three Marks are *impermanence, suffering, and egolessness.*

Impermanence is the concept that nothing lasts, everything will disintegrate eventually, and to deny this is to deny reality. Both good and bad are destined to pass soon enough. Life is in a constant state of flux. This plays out in your thoughts and mental states, as well as a simultaneously decaying and growing world around you.

Unhappiness stems from attachment and clinging to what is good, denying that it is impermanent. We are creating our own sorrows, yet we don't realize it.

Suffering is the concept that all experiences and thoughts contain a pinch of suffering, whether directly or only indirectly. Due to the impermanent nature of life, nothing will ever bring us lasting happiness, and our happiness is always destined to swing toward unhappiness at some point. Even when we are happy, we are in a state of pre-suffering and dread. Every step we take toward happiness simply brings the unhappiness afterward that much closer.

Egolessness is the concept that there is no *you*; *you* is simply the product of your perceptions, thoughts, surroundings, and consciousness. Each of these ingredients changes every moment, which means that your identity does not exist in the traditional sense. Your identity is rooted in the current moment, yet we cling to our past experiences and narratives that give us expectations that are not current and not warranted. This clinging keeps us from enjoying the present moment.

The overall message of the Three Marks of Existence is that we are perpetually unable to let go. We deny each of the three marks; we deny impermanence when we are happy, we deny suffering as a vital aspect of existence, and we deny egolessness because we hold onto our identity and subsequent expectations. They are universal aspects of every human life. This leads directly to what Buddha saw as the true root causes of suffering encompassed in the Four Noble Truths.

The Problem: the Four Noble Truths

For Buddha, the path to happiness starts from an understanding of the root causes of suffering. Some might consider Buddha a pessimist because of his obsession with suffering, but that is missing his intention. At this point, he is more like a doctor—to develop an effective treatment, he must first articulate the problem, and then he can prescribe a proactive course of treatment later on. In fact, this is the *only* way that we can move forward. The Eightfold Path is this course of treatment.

During his meditations under the Bodhi tree, Buddha clearly articulated that which makes us unhappy—the symptoms that the Eightfold Path are meant to address and rectify with time and effort. Meditation is, of course, the most well-known tool of this practice, but contrary to popular belief, it is not about detaching from the world. Rather, it is a tool to train the mind not to dwell in the past or the future, but to live in the here and now, the realm in which we can experience peace most readily.

But first and foremost, what are the problems to be addressed?

Noble Truth #1: Life is suffering.

Life always involves suffering, in obvious and subtle forms. Even when things seem good, we always feel an undercurrent of anxiety and uncertainty inside. The first noble truth is sometimes translated as "life is stressful," which may resonate a little more with you.

This suffering encompasses the obvious forms of pain, illness, and trauma we can all imagine, such as a broken arm, viral sickness, or death of a loved one. It also includes milder forms of discomfort and distress, like long hours of work, feeling let down by a partner, a headache, feeling frustrated, disappointed, hurt, inadequate, depressed, upset, etc.

Suffering even includes the subtlest tension in the mind, restlessness, a sense of preoccupation, unease, or boredom, a sense of lacking, and so on. They may not all come to mind when we think of suffering, but they are all squarely on the negative side of the spectrum.

The Buddha was not saying that everything about life is relentlessly awful. Happiness certainly exists and is an integral aspect of living. But as we look more closely at suffering, we see that it touches everything in our lives, including good fortune and happy times, because everything is temporary and passing.

Noble Truth #2: Suffering comes from desiring.

The cause of suffering is craving, attachment, and desiring. We suffer because of the narrow and large gaps between what we want and what we receive. This even happens once we receive what we thought we wanted. As we achieve what we desire, we grow lustful and want even more. And so the vicious circle continues. No matter how successful we are, we never remain satisfied.

We seek out and attach ourselves to material objects, titles, and honors. These arbitrary (and often intangible) concepts hold great power over us, and we grow frustrated when the world doesn't behave the way we think it should and our lives don't conform to our expectations. We seek satisfaction from external sources, and this is a never-ending carousel that will forever keep you wanting more.

We all desire and want; this is natural and unavoidable. Buddha simply meant that we cannot become slaves to our desires, such that they hold our happiness hostage.

This means we must give up the *attachment* we have to certain outcomes and rewards. It is our staunch dedication to them that creates our suffering or stress. Desiring and wanting without such attachment to what the end result is can and will lead to happiness. This leads directly to the third truth.

Noble Truth #3: Letting go ends suffering.

The solution to suffering is to let go of your attachments. But how do we do that? The fact is that you can't by an act of will. It's impossible to just prohibit yourself from attaching to the result that you desire. We can consciously and logically know what we must do, but our emotions and unconscious minds don't usually follow suit so neatly. In short, the conditions that create attachment will still be present.

The Second Noble Truth tells us that we are attached to outcomes that will make us happy. This means, by definition, we are looking for external sources of fulfillment, and to boot, they are all impermanent anyway. It is only when we see this for ourselves that we can stop grasping. When we do see it, the letting go is easy. The craving will seem to disappear of its own accord.

This doesn't seem particularly helpful, other than to propose that liberation from desires is indeed possible. But that's what the next section on the Eightfold Path is about.

Noble Truth #4: There is a way.

The Buddha spent the last 45 or so years of his life speaking on aspects of the Four Noble Truths. The majority of these were about the fourth truth: the Eightfold Path.

Remember, the Buddha's purpose with the Four Noble Truths was to set the grounds for which our treatment would come: the Eightfold Path. Unlike in many other religions, Buddhism has no particular benefit to merely believing in a doctrine. Instead, the emphasis is on living the doctrine and walking the path, because that is the only thing that will alleviate attachment and suffering.

The path is eight broad areas of practice that touch every part of our lives. It ranges from study to ethical conduct, what you do for a living, and how you should think from moment to moment. Every action of body, speech, and mind are addressed. It is a path of exploration and discipline to be walked for the rest of one's life. It is thorough to say the least.

Without the path, the first three truths would just be a theory on suffering—similar to the theory of heliocentrism, where philosophers and scientists could only argue about it. The Eightfold Path brings the true meaning of Buddhism and nirvana into one's life.

The Solution: The Eightfold Path

Buddha described the Eightfold Path as the way that leads to the uprooting of the causes of suffering and thus to increasingly stable and profound peacefulness, wisdom, virtue, and happiness. It is the path to everything we want out of life because it makes us happier with less or even nothing.

Each of the elements of this Path is described by a word that is typically translated as "right" or "wise." Both meanings are useful to reflect upon. Each element of the path is *right* in the sense of being correct, moral, and a specific instruction about how to live. Each element is also *wise* in the sense of resulting from deep understanding and leading to good results.

While the eight elements of the path are presented here in their traditional sequence, they are not something you develop in order. They are all important, all the time, all at once. Yet some may become more prominent aspects of your practice at one time or another.

Remember that each element's overall purpose is to cease attachment and thus suffering. Knowledge itself is not enough; the path must be walked. It is called a *path* for a reason.

The Eightfold Path is a practical and systematic way to eliminate attachment and dissatisfaction from our minds and our lifestyle through mindful thoughts and actions. In brief, the eight elements of the path are outlined below:

(1) Right Understanding: an accurate understanding of the nature of the

universe, specifically the Four Noble Truths.

(2) Right Intentions: avoiding thoughts of attachment, hatred, and negativity.

(3) Right Speech: refraining from verbal misbehavior such as lying, argumentation, insults, speaking without thinking, and harshness.

(4) Right Action: refraining from physical misbehavior such as stealing, killing, harming others, and sexual misdeeds.

(5) Right Livelihood: avoiding occupations that harm others in some way, such as selling slaves, weapons, animals, intoxicants, or drugs.

(6) Right Effort: abandoning negative mindsets, preventing negative mindsets in the future, and retaining positive mindsets.

(7) Right Mindfulness: practicing awareness of your body, feelings, and thoughts.

(8) Right Concentration: practicing meditation and achieving single-mindedness and focus.

Right Understanding: This requires clear and deep comprehension of the Four Noble

Truths and Three Marks of Existence. To understand those aspects is to truly know attachment's role in suffering and unhappiness. In fact, suffering is manmade and arises only as a result of your perception. It would not be inaccurate to understand that suffering is only as real or illusory as you want to make it.

Right Intentions: With right thoughts, right actions follow. Everything begins with our intentions. Sometimes, this is translated as "Right Thoughts." In this context, thoughts mold our actions and character. Unhelpful thoughts will lead to unhappiness, while the right thoughts will lead to a ceasing of attachment. There are three specific types of intentions that we must do our best to focus on:

- Renunciation (Nekkhamma) of pleasure and becoming selfless as opposed to selfish and desirous.
- Loving (Metta) or goodwill toward everyone, including yourself, as opposed to hatred, jealousy, spite, and indifference.

- Harmlessness (Avihimsa) or compassion as opposed to cruelty and lack of empathy.

Right Speech: Our words follow our intentions, most of the time. But sometimes it works in reverse. The words you choose create the world around you. And this is entirely within your control. If you are swearing, judging, or being abusive, your thoughts will certainly match your speech, and vice versa. Just try to avoid speaking negativity into existence.

Right Action: With good intentions and filtered speech, next, your actions have to be compatible. There are obvious actions to avoid, such as killing, violence, stealing, and so on. With these first three steps on the Eightfold Path, we can gradually eliminate bad tendencies from our lives.

Right Livelihood: As long as you don't do harm to others, and that includes the environment, since that impacts all beings, then it's Right Livelihood. It should be fairly obvious that any attempt at purifying intentions, speech, and actions is impossible if your occupation indirectly does harm to others. A few specific examples are listed: creating weapons, slavery, breeding animals for slaughter, illegal drugs, and producing poisons to both humans and the environment.

Right Effort: To do anything in life requires effort. Nothing you want is easy. Determination, persistence, and energy are needed to walk the Eightfold Path. Right effort includes developing good habits, such as practicing right mindfulness, right meditation, and other positive moral acts in your daily life. You must devote yourself to these practices.

Right Mindfulness: This is the constant observation of your own intentions, speech, feelings, body, and thoughts. It is gaining self-awareness of everything, especially the attachments you possess. Without mindfulness, you are unable to follow the Eightfold Path. It enables you to catch and eliminate subconscious mental/verbal/physical actions that are negative or bad.

We often don't know why we react or what we feel. Through right mindfulness, one can free oneself from passions and cravings, which so often make us prisoners of past regrets or future preoccupations.

Right Concentration: The purpose is to train your mind to obey you and not the other way around. This is where the practice of meditation comes into play.

When you start practicing meditation, you will be shocked at how difficult a little bit of regulation and control on your mind is. It is indeed the chattering monkey brain because it never ceases and never relaxes. All sorts of thoughts will go on in your mind. Initially, it will be like riding a wild horse without getting thrown off. But with strength and determination, you will gradually gain a sense of deep focus and concentration. There are many paths to this type of mental calm, but one prominent method is to focus on observing yourself. Don't have thoughts about what you are seeing or thinking or feeling—simply observe it as it happens. Stay in the present, mindfully watching and observing.

According to Buddha, there are four stages of deeper concentration.

(1) The first stage of concentration is one in which mental hindrances and impure intentions disappear and a sense of bliss is achieved. (2) In the second stage, activities of the mind come to an end and only bliss remains. (3) In the third stage, bliss itself begins to disappear. (4) In the final stage, all sensations including bliss disappear and are replaced by a total peace of mind, which Buddha described as a deeper sense of happiness.

Once you have succeeded in focusing your mind on a point, you can direct it like a laser pointer. This is how you transform your mind to destroy attachment and suffering.

The Art of Letting Go

Although a very clear blueprint was laid out by Buddha, however, in practical terms, the art of letting go may be simple, but it is not easy.

Attachment comes into our lives in small and unexpected ways—for instance, any time we have any expectation, no matter how well-grounded or justified it may be. This is an attachment to an outcome or reward. And any time there is a mismatch, the friction will cause suffering of your very own doing. Suffering is the gap between what you want and what occurs. We cannot always control what occurs, but we can and should control our attachment to what we want.

New attachments will always threaten to derail you, but recognize how impermanent they are. When you stop trying to grasp, own, and control the world around you, you give it the freedom to fulfill you without the power to destroy you. That's why letting go is so important—letting go is letting happiness in.

It's no simple undertaking to let go of attachment—not a one-time decision, like pulling off a Band-Aid. Instead, it's a day-to-day, moment-to-moment commitment that involves changing the way you experience and interact with everything you instinctively want to hold on to.

Accept the moment for what it is. Yesterday is gone, and you can't do anything about it. The present moment is here, and you can't change it; enjoy it if it is positive, and know that it will quickly pass if it is negative. The future is not yet here, so it is pointless to think about. Don't fight or resist the current reality; just embrace it and make sure you try to extract as much as possible from it.

When you place your expectations on external things rather than your own mindset, you are setting yourself up for failure. Rather, you need to simply allow things to happen. Allow negativity and the ensuing emotions, and then allow yourself to detach and move on. The world does not conform to our "shoulds" and "musts"; at best, it provides incredibly uncertain guarantees. We cannot control this.

But in the end, this too shall pass. Look around you; everything you see will pass and disintegrate into nothingness. Keep some perspective in mind; it is this same recognition of impermanence that will help you let go and detach.

Takeaways:

- Our conventional view of Buddhism is that it's about giving up all of your material possessions and joining a monastery. While misguided, this speaks to the central tenet of Buddhism: ceasing attachments.
- Buddhism as a life philosophy is quite instructive because it lays out a premise, a problem, and a clear solution to the problem. The premise is the Three Marks of Existence, which describe the realities of human beings: everything is impermanent, life is suffering, and who

you are changes from moment to moment.

- The problem is the Four Noble Truths, which stem from the Three Marks of Existence, which describe why humans are unhappy as well as the key to overcoming it. They are: life is suffering, suffering comes from attachment, letting go of attachment ends suffering, and the Eightfold Path is the way to happiness.
- The solution is the Eightfold Path, which is a series of eight large and small actions to perform to achieve enlightenment and freedom from attachment. They must be embodied, not simply ruminated over. The purpose is to create a sense of enlightenment and freedom from attachment by living the right way. They are: right understanding, right intentions, right speech, right action, right livelihood, right effort, right mindfulness, and right concentration.

Chapter 4. Descartes and Seeking Absolute Truth

The Frenchman Rene Descartes is generally considered the founder of modern Western philosophy. It's a lofty title, but the magnitude of work he put forth in his life speaks for itself. Western European academics and philosophers at the time of his life (1596–1650) generally rushed to respond to his multitude of ideas, and that formed the backbone of the Enlightenment period of humanity.

What was his main contribution, for the purposes of this book, on creating a personal life philosophy? Stubborn doubt and adhering to a simple mandate of the pursuit of truth. Oh, and not believing the thinkers who came before him.

Just because something was stated to be true did not mean it was because he was unable to either observe or reason it for himself. You can now imagine why his thoughts left other philosophers rushing to respond—because he upended literal centuries of thought.

And so eventually Descartes became known for his stances on doubt and not believing dogma for dogma's sake. He required proper examination and analysis; only from there could you be sure that you weren't building your knowledge on a house of cards.

The following words have sometimes also been used to describe his approach to thought: doubt, skepticism, distrust, and rationalism. All he wanted to do was discover and understand.

You could see this as not trusting in others, but rather, it was his way of gaining a sense of *certainty*. Without certainty in what we are saying through proof or experience, nothing can be taken as truth. And truth is all Descartes ever wanted.

He suggests that it is pointless to claim that something is real or exists unless we first know how such a claim could be known as a justified true belief. But to say that our beliefs are justified, we have to be able to base them ultimately on a belief that is itself indubitable. Such a belief could then provide a firm foundation on which all subsequent beliefs are grounded and could thus be known as true. But how could we know that those beliefs are grounded and true? It seems like it could devolve into circular thinking, but those final beliefs must be based on what is provable or observable. Essentially, Descartes prompts a chain of asking "But how do you know?" until you can point to a direct experience or real evidence.

Can you think of a highly popular institution that this approach might conflict with, especially with events like the Spanish

Inquisition burning people for heresy barely a century past? That's right: religion, which tends to be based on faith and the very absence of proof, which is an intentional aspect, not a shortcoming.

Although Descartes remained a committed Catholic throughout his life, you can imagine how controversial his writings were for the time. For reference, his contemporary Galileo Galilei was famously found guilty of heresy by the Catholic Church for his views on how the earth revolved around the sun—in 1633.

Ironically, Descartes' method of doubting was aimed at defending the Catholic faith and using reasoning and logic to confirm the truth of the religion. However, the Enlightenment marked an erosion of the Church's authority and influence, so perhaps Descartes had the opposite effect that he intended.

This brings us to where Descartes can help inform our life philosophy. He brings together elements of critical thinking, healthy skepticism, and doubt to ensure that we are seeing reality for what it is. Descartes can help us find the truth in everyday life just by shifting our perspective to one of slight doubt. It's not to say that you shouldn't be trusting, but simply reserving judgment at first is a powerful weapon in seeking happiness and making fulfilling decisions.

It's a life philosophy of caution, looking before you leap, and measured decisions. Some others might possess the philosophy of "never saying no" or *carpe diem* ("seize the day")—that's a different matter. You can still do those things, but first understand what the truth of the matter is.

In 1637, he published one of his most important works, including *Discours de la method*, but he published the main topic of this chapter on seeking absolute truth in 1641: *Meditations on First Philosophy*.

In it, Descartes discusses how we are able to check our beliefs against reality by essentially the first version of the scientific method. It consists of six meditations (we will only focus on the first three) about the proper method of philosophical reflection, proof, and the conclusions that can be drawn. Throughout, Descartes insists that (1) we can claim to know only that for which we have justification and (2) we must judge our ideas using a method that guarantees that our ideas are correct and justified.

Here's something of a table of contents for *Meditations on First Philosophy*:

- Meditation 1: Use the Method of Doubt to rid himself of all beliefs that could be false.
- Meditation 2: Arrive at some beliefs that could not possibly be false and thus must be true.
- Meditation 3: Articulate criteria for true knowledge.
- Meditation 4: Prove that the mind is distinct from the body.
- Meditation 5: Prove the existence of God.

- Meditation 6: Prove the existence of the external, physical world.

As mentioned, we'll only cover the first three meditations; from the titles, it is probably apparent why this is the case. They are the meditations more directly concerned with finding truth and living life through a lens of critical thinking. The first three meditations work together sequentially through a sort of process of elimination. First, you eliminate falsehoods. Second, you sort through what's left. Third, you make a judgment based on what you find. It's a methodical way of thinking that, if applied correctly, allows you to understand the world better.

We'll go through each of the three meditations in detail.

Meditation 1

In his first *Meditation,* Descartes focuses on distinguishing between what is true and false.

To complicate matters, the fact that you have experienced something does not mean it is true. This is because of our senses, prejudices, biases, or perceptions. Everyone has their own version of truth, but that is not *the* truth. In order to test whether what we think we know is truly correct, Descartes suggests that we adopt a method that will avoid error by tracing what we know back to a foundation of indubitable beliefs. We have to challenge what we've always held to be true and doubt everything we know.

Such a radical flip might seem unreasonable, and Descartes certainly does not mean that we really should doubt everything in our lives, from our names to our heritage. He simply suggests that we should temporarily pretend that everything we know is questionable.

This is called *hypothetical doubt*, and we should hold such doubt regarding (1) the perceptions of our senses toward our experiences and (2) our reasoning abilities. As Descartes puts it,

But inasmuch as reason already persuades me that I ought no less carefully to withhold my assent from matters which are not entirely certain and indubitable than from those which appear to me manifestly to be false, if I am able to find in each one some reason to doubt, this will suffice to justify my rejecting the whole. And for that end it will not be requisite that I should examine each in particular, which would be an endless undertaking; for owing to the fact that the destruction of the foundations of necessity brings with it the downfall of the rest of the edifice, I shall only in the first place attack those principles upon which all my former opinions rested.

Translation?

Descartes was the ultimate naysayer and contrarian. So he made the decision that he would no longer hold beliefs that had the slightest amount of doubt surrounding them. Logically, this would lead to knowledge and truth that was absolute. Practically speaking, this would be troublesome at best, but this was the essence of Descartes' famous method of doubt, the process of which will soon be articulated.

He recognized the impracticality of disavowing all the knowledge he had been taught and even observed (the sky is blue, right?), so he created broad categories of beliefs.

The first category consisted of beliefs that he had learned through his own senses. Surprisingly, he considered that the senses did not impart absolute truth. You can see that the sky is blue; everyone can observe the same thing, right? Not exactly.

> All that up to the present time I have accepted as most true and certain I have learned either from the senses or through the senses; but it is sometimes proved to me that these senses are deceptive, and it is wiser not to trust entirely to anything by

which we have once been deceived...
on many occasions I have in sleep
been deceived by similar illusions,
and in dwelling carefully on this
reflection I see so manifestly that
there are no certain indications by
which we may clearly distinguish
wakefulness from sleep that I am lost
in astonishment.

We do not know that what we experience
through our senses is true; at least, we are
not certain of it. And we cannot tell when
our senses are correctly reporting the way
things really are and when they are not. So
the best thing to do is to doubt whether any
knowledge can be based on our sense
experiences. Descartes didn't believe his
senses, and this is best exemplified in his
analysis of dreams.

In a nutshell, dreams lead to a certain type
of experience, yet they do not represent
reality. But it is often impossible to
distinguish between dream experiences and
waking, real-life experiences. Therefore,

this experience is not a reliable source of truth and knowledge.

Descartes is not saying that we are merely dreaming all that we experience, nor is he saying that we cannot distinguish dreaming from being awake. His point is that we cannot be sure that what we experience as being real in the world is actually real.

Recall that the second portion of Descartes' method of doubt involved reason. This is to say that our reasoning abilities cannot always be trusted—this is a self-evident truth as we are always subject to cognitive biases, skewed perspectives, and simple errors. This is what is typically referred to as the *demon* problem, whereas earlier we had the *dream* problem.

> I shall then suppose, not that God who is supremely good and the fountain of truth, but some evil genius not less powerful than deceitful, has employed his whole energies in deceiving me; I shall consider that the heavens, the earth,

colours, figures, sound, and all other external things are nought but the illusions and dreams of which this genius has availed himself in order to lay traps for my credulity; I shall consider myself as having no hands, no eyes, no flesh, no blood, nor any senses, yet falsely believing myself to possess all these things; I shall remain obstinately attached to this idea, and if by this means it is not in my power to arrive at the knowledge of any truth, I may at least do what is in my power and with firm purpose avoid giving credence to any false thing, or being imposed upon by this arch deceiver, however powerful and deceptive he may be.

Translation? We can't be sure that our reasoning abilities are trustworthy, honest, reliable, or correct. Descartes puts forth an argument to prove his point, just like before. If we think about a simple addition problem such as 2+3=5, then there are two possibilities about how we reach the answer. The first possibility is that our powers of reasoning are indeed reliable and sound, and thus we are calculating correctly.

The second possibility is that an evil demon from the depths of the earth is manipulating our brain, and we only come to the conclusion that 2+3=5 because the demon puts that idea in our minds. Here, we come to an answer via deception and a profound lack of correct reasoning.

Thus, we can only trust our sense of reasoning if we can ensure that the second possibility, and ones like it, are never occurring. But that's not possible. We can't ensure that our sense of reasoning is reliable or absolute truth—not by itself anyway.

This can be a highly disconcerting notion— to not be able to trust your own reasoning and thought processes. If you can't trust your senses or thoughts, then in what sense is your view of the world real or accurate? What, if anything, can provide the type of certainty that Descartes so desires? That is the very conundrum Descartes dealt with and strove to fix.

Meditation 2

Meditation 1 was about ridding oneself of the beliefs that could be false, most notably from our senses and from our mental reasoning. Meditation 2 follows on that thread and is about finding beliefs that are true no matter what.

How does one find these propositions if we cannot trust our senses or reasoning? It was only from those propositions that you could build knowledge of the world that was reliable and true—only by working from a base of truth could you have the chance of concluding truth.

Obviously, the point was clear that he must attempt to find universal truths that were without a doubt correct. From this particular line of thought sprung one of the most famous lines in all of Western philosophy. But first, his inner dialogue:

But I was persuaded that there was nothing in all the world, that there was no heaven, no earth, that there were no minds, nor any bodies: was I not then likewise persuaded that I did not exist? Not at all; [surely] I myself did exist, since I persuaded myself of something. But there is some deceiver or other, very powerful and very cunning, who ever employs his ingenuity in deceiving me. Then without doubt I exist also if he deceives me, and let him deceive me as much as he will, he can never cause me to be nothing so long as I think that I am something. So that after having reflected well and carefully examined all things, we must come to the definite conclusion that this proposition, "I am, I exist," is necessarily true each time that I pronounce it, or that I mentally conceive it.

You may have guessed what's coming next.
"*I think; therefore, I exist*"
In Latin, "*Cogito ergo sum.*"

This sprang from Descartes' argument for a universal truth, winding its way around the first meditation's two major roadblocks of not trusting senses and reasoning. The fact that *he* is being deceived by a demon is something in itself. If there is a deception, it must be acting upon something, and that something is Descartes himself. Thus, an undeniable truth must be that he exists.

Descartes realizes that he cannot question his own existence because he is a "thinking thing." Even if he doubts the senses and the body, he cannot doubt himself because of his thoughts. Even if we were to be deceived by an evil demon as to what we see and hear, if the thoughts are still there, we would still exist.

But to further expound on what *cogito ergo sum* actually proves, it doesn't mean that he exists as a person, a soul, or a body. It simply speaks to the limited scope that because he thinks, he exists, and thus the undeniable truth is only that he is a thing that thinks. Whatever thinks exists.

Descartes thinks (albeit in a flawed way), and therefore he exists as a thinking thing.

It's almost the mental equivalent of a tongue twister. At this point, all Descartes has reasoned out is that he exists as a thinking being and there are no other things he knows for certain—not his name, his age, or the size of his bed.

Where can we go from here?

Meditation 3

> I am certain that I am a thinking thing; but do I not therefore likewise know what is required to render me certain of a truth? In this first knowledge, doubtless, there is nothing that gives me assurance of its truth except the clear and distinct perception of what I affirm, which would not indeed be sufficient to give me the assurance that what I say is true, if it could ever happen that anything I thus clearly and distinctly perceived should prove false; and

accordingly it seems to me that I may now take as a general rule, that *all that is very clearly and distinctly apprehended is true*.

Translation? Well, Descartes sets a new standard for what could be considered true knowledge almost without us realizing it: "clearly and distinctly apprehended." But what does that mean?

When we see something *clearly*, then our vision is unblocked—we have a clear view of the object in question. It is not too far away, it is not blurry, it is not too dark to make it out, and so on. When we see something *distinctly*, we are able to differentiate the object from all other objects. If we see a button among a pile of similar buttons, we do not see it distinctly— we can easily confuse it for one of the other buttons nearby.

In other words, clear and distinct perceptions are defined by Descartes as those perceptions that are so self-evident that, while they are held in the mind, they cannot logically be doubted.

Examples of clear and distinct perceptions include the propositions "A=A" and "I exist." All knowledge, according to Descartes, is supposed to proceed from clear and distinct perceptions; no proposition is supposed to be judged as true unless it is perceived clearly and distinctly. Clear and distinct ideas are formally known as basic or self-justifying beliefs that Descartes hoped to use as foundations for his system of knowledge.

Consider the proposition that 2+3=5. We can have a clear understanding of the proposition (unobscured by other thoughts, with a clear understanding of the different parts of the proposition and how they fit together). Also, we aren't going to confuse it with some other proposition (e.g., that 2+3=6).

You might feel that there are some gaps left in this definition of absolutely true knowledge, but that will be addressed shortly.

From what we know in *Meditations on First Philosophy* thus far, our senses and reasoning are unreliable, and then the only thing we can know is that we ourselves are a thing that thinks (because we are thinking right now). This allows us to infer that, since *cogito ergo sum* is clear and distinct, clear and distinct propositions are the base of true knowledge. Or does it?

How can we say that clear and distinct propositions are indeed the most basic truth that exists? How can we be prevented from going down a further rabbit hole when we know that our most basic thoughts and senses are unreliable? How do we know the demon can't corrupt our thoughts on A=A?

This is where Descartes' devout Catholicism comes into play, and perhaps he deviates from his stance of everything requiring hard evidence and proof. God is the ultimate arbiter of truth and knowledge. This is also one of the most common critiques of *Meditations on First Philosophy*, because it seems to be contradictory to the very point of not trusting your own beliefs or thoughts.

> But when I considered any matter in arithmetic and geometry, that was very simple and easy, as, for example, that two and three added together make five, and things of this sort, did I not view them with at least sufficient clearness to warrant me in affirming their truth? Indeed, if I afterward judged that we ought to doubt of these things, it was for no other reason than because it occurred to me that a God might perhaps have given me such a nature as that I should be deceived, even respecting the matters that appeared to me the most evidently true...And in truth, as I have no ground for believing that Deity is deceitful, ...the ground of doubt that rests only on this supposition is very slight, and, so to speak, metaphysical. But, that I may be able wholly to remove it, I

must inquire whether there is a God...and if I find that there is a God, I must examine likewise whether he can be a deceiver; for, *without the knowledge of these two truths, I do not see that I can ever be certain of anything.*

Translation? Descartes is worried that there might be a demon who has the power to confuse us or deceive us even about a very simple mathematical proposition, so there is the possibility that we only *think* we are being clear and distinct.

Certain propositions (*I doubt, I exist, I am a thinking thing*) are completely demon-proof. However, he has said that even simple mathematical propositions are not. Thus, he uses God as a foil to keep the third meditation flowing. There are universal truths, espoused and approved by God, that we can find, and they are essentially categorized as clear and distinct. It's arbitrary and not overly helpful in determining categories, but this does logically flow.

Anything that is not clear and distinct is said to be not demon-proof; thus, it cannot be absolute truth.

But if we get beyond the nitty-gritty details and steps of logic (some of it bordering on semantics and picking words apart), we are at the culmination of Descartes' view of knowledge and the world. From this limited scope, he intended to engage in what is known as *foundationalism*—finding truths that are built only upon preceding truths.

It's a way of looking at the world with absolute precision and skepticism. It's how a scientist might approach a stringent test with multiple variables, yet it was his key to understanding knowledge.

We don't have to approach life in such a systematic way, but we can certainly take some cues from Descartes about how to think and live better. Look before you leap, measure twice before cutting, and keep from jumping to conclusions. Challenge your thoughts, especially the ones that you consider engraved in stone. Don't let yourself be guided by others just because. Have a high standard for what you believe; this ensures that your actions will represent exactly what you want.

Another famous philosopher known for his doubt and questioning methods, Socrates, once stated that the unexamined life is not worth living. Adhering to Descartes' principles on doubt and truth will certainly get you into examining your life and gaining clarity into your own thoughts, desires, and motivations. That is perhaps the most powerful purpose of the chapter—if you don't doubt your own thoughts (at least sometimes) then you are in a world of your own creation, and not one rooted in truth and reality.

Takeaways:

- Rene Descartes helps us live a better life through embracing doubt and seeking to discover only the absolute truth. He upended centuries of philosophical and scientific thought with this simple notion. His thoughts on the matter came to a head in his book *Meditations on First Philosophy*, which contains six meditations. The first three are more relevant to our purposes of finding truth and gaining certainty that our belief *is* the truth. The first three meditations are part of a process of finding what is true.

- Meditation 1 is about knowing that our beliefs are potentially flawed in two main ways: our sensations can lie to us, and our reasoning can be incorrect. Descartes poked holes in just about everything we know using the dream problem and the demon problem. The dream problem supposes that since our senses are the same when we dream, we cannot rely on them to tell the truth. The demon problem supposes that a demon could be feeding us our reasoning, and thus we can't be sure that it is the truth. So once we understand that much of what we think is not necessarily true, we move onto the next step.

- Meditation 2 is about finding beliefs that are absolutely true, and for this, Descartes turns to one of the most famous thought experiments: *cogito ergo sum*. This of course means "I think; therefore, I am." Despite demons or dreams, because Descartes has made a thought, it means he exists. This was his process of finding an absolute truth through logic. It was the most basic starting place to build from.

- Meditation 3 follows on Meditation 2's assertion of truth. From *cogito ergo sum*, Descartes suggests the standard for truth is that which is *clear and distinct*. This is a relatively hazy definition, and he makes it clear later on that he considers the word of God to be clear and distinct. Remember, one of his main goals for doubt was to gain greater confidence in the existence of God. But don't let his methods of doubt for finding truth be obscured by this last step.
- Understand that which can be false (most beliefs). Second, find a method for proving the truth of a matter. This is a mindset that can be applied to nearly every aspect of your life; it can ensure that you aren't being suckered or

laboring under falsehoods. When you are sure about what you know, then your actions can follow your intentions.

Chapter 5. Confucius and the Five Relationships

Confucianism is China; China is Confucianism.

This is no mistake, rather a deliberate process over time. Although Confucius's writings were never intended to be a cultural guide, rather a political treatise, they have been strongly intertwined with Chinese (and adjacent) culture for centuries.

As in every country, there are good actors and bad actors, but the fact that China and other East Asian countries can be categorized as collectivistic rather than individualistic speaks to the influence of

Confucius. For well over a billion people to unconsciously adhere to these values, you must figure that there is something in his writings that helps provide guidance in the way of a life philosophy.

All that remains are thoughts on how to live, with little regard to the religious aspect that it once held. In fact, Confucianism is quite humanistic in its emphasis on the ordinary activities of humans. With the goal of achieving fulfillment, this is probably more practical because it places the power in our hands.

Confucius was born in 551 BC and began to work as a teacher but eventually transitioned to working in government. By the time he was 50 years old, he held a high position, and just as swiftly as his ascent, he was reputedly pushed out of office only five years later due to rivals and enemies.

During the next 12 years, Confucius wandered from place to place with a few of his disciples. He was jeered at and even placed in jail. At the age of 67, he found himself as an advisor to the Duke of Ai. During the next years, he spent his time teaching and compiling some of the classic Chinese texts. He died in 479 BC. By the sixth century AD, every prefecture in China had a temple to honor Confucius.

How did he attain such wide acclaim? Shortly after his death, his disciples compiled a work known as the *Lun yü,* commonly translated as the *Analects* but more accurately called the *Edited Conversations*. This work consists of conversations between Confucius and his students.

The primary emphasis of the *Lun yü* is political philosophy. Confucius taught that the primary task of the ruler was to achieve the well-being and happiness of his people. To accomplish this aim, the ruler first had to set a moral (good character) example by his own conduct. This example would in turn influence the people's behavior, as societal values stemmed from the politics at the top. It eventually trickled down into all levels of the Chinese people.

A Cultural Philosophy: The Five Relationships

Even though he quit his job as a teacher, Confucius ended up as one of the greatest teachers in Chinese history. He died far before his influence was ever widely felt, but his disciples spread his theories for centuries until, in the first Han dynasty (206 BC to 8 AD), they became the basis of the state ideology, the bundle of ideas identifying the social needs of a culture. Confucianism focuses on human conduct toward other humans, not religious belief or a natural flow. Living better is a result of treating others properly and in specific ways befitting their position—two distinct behaviors in Confucianism.

Confucianism is a worldview, set of ethics, political ideology, and way of life. Sometimes viewed as a philosophy and sometimes as a religion, Confucianism focuses on people first.

Both the theory and practice of Confucianism have indelibly marked the patterns of government, society, education, and familial bonds of East Asia. Confucian mindsets have been the most basic mainstream value of the common people of the Han Chinese nationality and other nationalities in China from antiquity to the modern day. The basic values and virtues of Confucian thoughts are the unconscious rules that govern daily conduct for most Chinese people, most of the time.

All you have to do is think about the soft-spoken and passive stereotype you might have heard about East Asians: eager to please, incredibly hospitable, and horrifically avoidant of confrontation. These are all consequences of a Confucian way of thought. The harmony of the many must supersede the harmony of the single person, and to cause discord is to ignore the five relationships or the five virtues. It can seem fairly restrictive, and in some ways, it is—if you're not used to it. If you're used to it, then you simply know that your own happiness is not your priority; your happiness comes from upholding and improving society.

As mentioned, Confucius was mainly interested in how to bring about societal order and harmony for the goal of effective governance. He believed that mankind would be in harmony with the universe if everyone understood their rank in society and were taught the proper behaviors of their rank. Similarly, he believed that the social order was threatened whenever people failed to act according to their prescribed roles.

This almost starts to sound like a caste system or communist world order, but his ideal society functioned smoothly because everyone recognized who they were and didn't try to be someone they were not. There were specific dynamics to always keep in mind. You have to know your proper role, as well as how to act within it. If it doesn't sound like it has a caste system tendency, then it may begin to sound like it is trapping you into a series of dishonest formalities. But to Confucius, that would be you prioritizing yourself over society. In an ideal world existing in a vacuum, this is perhaps easier to envision.

Confucius devised a system of interdependent relationships—a structure in which the lower level gives obedience to the higher level (extending from the family level to the national). As a result, Chinese culture tends to give a considerable amount of reverence for authority and age (though not necessarily sincere, especially in modern China).

He believed that moral behavior stemmed from the fulfillment of traditional roles, as defined by these five principal relationships, all of them with a subordinate/superior dynamic, with loyalty between friends as the only horizontal relationship. The dominant person receives respect and obedience from the subordinate person but is by no means a dictator. He is supposed to reciprocate with love, goodwill, support, and affection toward the subordinate person.

Take note that three of the five important relationships concern the nuclear family.

1. Ruler and subject. Show loyalty and trust in the ruler's guidance and direction. Give deference to their judgment and give them the benefit of the doubt. The ruler must demonstrate a good and moral example.
2. Father and son (parent to child). Show filialpiety. Filialpiety is the Confucian concept of powerful loyalty and deference to one's parents, elders, and ancestors. This translates into obedience, gratitude, and caretaking, based on the sacrifice that parents have made for their children. It can be fairly extreme at times and is a massive departure from the freedom from expectations that Westerners possess.
3. Elder brother and younger brother (siblings). Show brotherliness and friendship. But beyond that, there are elements of the parent to child relationship, where the elder brother must teach and set a proper example for the younger brother. The younger brother should not bring shame to the family.

4. Husband and wife (spouses). Show love, obedience, and honor. The husband must provide for the family while the wife must comply and handle other duties. Obviously, this relationship needs a retrofitting for modern societies, but properly honoring your spouse should go without saying.
5. Friend and friend. Show faithfulness. Be a good, reliable friend and show respect to each other. Help each other grow and become more moral and virtuous.

In one sense, the Confucian ethic is egalitarian, though not in a Western sense where everyone has equal standing and opportunity within society. Instead, there's equality within a social rank.

Though modern China has moved past these narrowly defined roles, Chinese today are still used to thinking in terms of hierarchy. They tend to respect hierarchy and differences in status much more than Westerners, who tend to be more egalitarian and open toward strangers.

In other words, in a Confucian society, you're supposed to act according to your rank, and not necessarily by how you feel. In the interest of social harmony, it was important to behave with reverence and obedience according to your rank. Indeed, it was not just the polite thing to do in traditional Chinese society. Saying the wrong thing to the emperor or a powerful official could literally cost you your life.

Even in modern China today, this cultural tendency to retain a more neutral public face still endures—especially in work situations and when dealing with those in authority.

It's probably obvious, but Western cultures tend to emphasize the individual—people are defined more by what they've accomplished than by group membership. Individual expression is encouraged from an early age and culturally reinforced in in the West.

In contrast, collectivism is inherent in a Confucian society. In order for Chinese society to operate smoothly, it is necessary to subject one's own desires to the greater good of the group. People don't exist independently of one another. Instead, an individual was defined by his or her relationship to the group. There is far more emphasis on social order and sacrificing oneself for these relationships, rather than on individual ambitions more common in Western cultures.

For millennia, the Chinese have been culturally conditioned to suppress personal needs and think in terms of collective responsibility—first, to their families, then community, clan, and nation at large.

Confucius was not interested in individual salvation or individual rights. What he cared about most was the collective well-being of society. Everything he did was in pursuit of that. But of course, for it to work, everyone involved has to agree and buy in; otherwise, the system won't work and will crumble.

At first glance, it seems that Confucianism certainly isn't something that will help you find your happiness. How can you be happy if you must constantly tend to the people around you, worrying that you might lose face or violate a boundary?

Instead of feeling a burden, consider Confucius's main message: to invest in your relationships.

Simple awareness of these five relationships to start with may lead you to reconsider how much investment you are giving to the people in your life. While this isn't a life philosophy in itself, it's well-known that relationships are the biggest source of happiness and fulfillment. Do unto others as you would have them do to you, and suddenly everything else in your life seems to take on a brighter light.

By contrast, you may realize that you are ignoring the important relationships in your life and causing inevitable discord and unhappiness. There are also different types of relationships and dynamics you should pay attention to; we have different responsibilities to certain people. Be more social, engage in society, and keep yourself deeply in touch with others. Don't allow yourself to become isolated.

In the end, the message is to spend much more time intentionally thinking about your relationships, as they ultimately determine your level of happiness.

Confucianism provides one other large concept toward better living: the five virtues (though sometimes four or six are articulated). Similar to Aristotle's virtues, these can function like a code of behavior in becoming a better person and living better. Of course, his virtues came a few hundred years before Aristotle's.

The Five Virtues

These virtues are the principles by which a person should live, according to Confucius. If a person embodies these virtues, he will be worthy of being called "the ideal person" or the "perfect person." And of course the ideal person receives only positive rewards of happiness.

Li: Li is the principle of self-restraint and sense of propriety. A person should always act in an honorable way and respect his elders, his ancestors, and his family members. He shall not be selfish in his acts. It does not mean that he should not have personal ambitions and aspirations, but he should not achieve them by being unjust to others. It includes following social etiquette and mannerisms. Pay heed to the five relationships and fit into society at large.

Behave how you are supposed to behave, essentially. Respect your community and your responsibilities and duties as a human within it.

Yi: Yi is the principle of righteousness. It is upholding what is right and moral above everything else and sacrificing oneself for it, if need be. This includes sacrificing yourself and your own ambitions to fit into society and respect the five relationships. There are elements of self-restraint and being bound by duty.

Act with values and ethics, and you will become a person with righteousness.

Xin: Xin is the principle of honesty in life. Being honest with oneself and being honest with the people around you build trust and confidence. Match your words with your actions.

Ren: Ren is the most important of all principles. It means being kind and humane to your fellow beings. Share and understand each other without being judgmental. Even if a person behaves badly with you, think about the condition he is in and what is making him behave this way. Help each other out and be generous. Give people the benefit of the doubt. When you realize how important society is over the individual, and how the five relationships reinforce that, you'll see that this particular virtue is without a doubt the cornerstone of the virtues. It succinctly states, "What one does not wish for oneself, one ought not to do to anyone else; what one recognizes as desirable for oneself, one ought to be willing to grant to others."

Zhi: *Zhi* is the character and wisdom of a person. But this is something that needs to continually improve and develop.

The individual acquires *zhi* through education. The meaning of *zhi* is "native substance" or "basic stuff" relating to building character traits through learning and practice. Human beings are not born with moral goodness or evilness.

In a sense, *zhi* precedes the other virtues because without wisdom, one will probably not be able to develop a sense of ethics, social skills, or even just the plain common sense for the other virtues.

The five virtues end up being a lesser lesson in Confucianism's pursuit of happiness and harmony—emphasis on the latter.

Society is prioritized within Confucianism, and the philosophy reflects it. Looking at the research surrounding relationships and happiness, this is also good advice. People who are members of clubs, churches, and other organizations are happier, people who have a job are happier, and so on. The evidence shows that this is also true at a societal level.

Countries in which people have the densest networks of friends are also those in which people are the happiest. Often, these countries overlap with the lowest salaries and relative spending power—but that doesn't seem to make a difference. Focus on five specific relationships and mercilessly cut out the rest.

In comparison, Taoism says retreat to nature and Buddhism says withdraw from attachment—both these points of view are tricky if happiness is your goal. Happiness without a doubt comes from people, but those relationships don't just magically appear. They must be properly cultivated, and in this way, Confucius saw the path to happiness—if not for you, for the greater good. It is utilitarian in a sense. Invest in your relationships and friendships and seek to create harmony through demonstrating the five virtues.

Takeaways:

- Confucianism, despite the intention, has been an integral part of Chinese and East Asian culture for centuries. Although Confucius was not necessarily greatly celebrated in his own lifetime, his teachings became official state doctrine hundreds of years after his death. It starts with the premise that the harmony of society is more important than almost any individual need, and everything else springs out of that. It may seem counterintuitive that a philosophy so focused on others can bring us happiness, but it simply reminds us of our roles and adjusts our expectations.
- The main aspect of Confucianism as it pertains to a life philosophy is the emphasis on the five relationships. Confucius believed that our adherence to specific roles in specific relationships

created a harmonious society and made our place within it harmonious and happy as well. It is noteworthy that three of the relationships relate to immediate family. The five relationships are ruler and subject, father and son, elder brother and younger brother, husband and wife, and friend and friend. The first four relationships all have a power dynamic, and as a result, deference is expected.

- The other aspect of Confucianism is the five Confucian virtues. They speak to self-restraint and propriety, righteousness, honesty, love of your fellow man, and wisdom and character. These ultimately have the same impact as Aristotle's virtues—a good blueprint or code of behavior to shoot for. Act accordingly and you will only be rewarded.

Chapter 6. Marcus Aurelius and Embracing Discomfort

Despite the name, Stoicism is not a life philosophy about ignoring your emotions and keeping up the appearance of being unaffected in the face of hardship.

The Stoics are often construed as cold, stone-like figures, but this is a misconception. In actuality, the Stoics had the full range of emotion that we all do, but they chose to focus on positive ones and let negative ones run their course.

The basic aim of Stoicism is to live in accordance with the flow of nature. Nature is unstoppable as well as unpredictable. We can't predict the future, and we can't prepare for every foreseeable outcome. Yet we must adapt and react to whatever comes our way somehow. We must still persist. We must thrive, even, in the face of hardship. How is that possible?

Most of the Western world in antiquity once was ruled by a Stoic: the eponymous Marcus Aurelius, emperor of Rome from 161–180 AD, who was often referred to as the philosopher king for his writings. Most of our conception of modern Stoicism comes from his diary, later turned into a book, *Meditations*.

Stoicism is not a religion, though at times it bears striking resemblances to some— Taoism for instance, which you'll read about next. But that's only because the end goals are the same, and as it turns out, there are only so many ways to peace, fulfillment, and harmony. Stoicism, however, is a direct system of thoughts for living better—that is the sole purpose, and it is unencumbered by having to pay tribute to a deity or set of spiritual beliefs. Stoicism is a way of living that places your fate into your own two hands.

Above all, Stoicism teaches the path of mental control to living a good life. Perhaps ironically this is done in large part by recognizing that we have control over very little in our lives except for our thoughts themselves. When we let go of the fantasy that we can control life, we can better deal with whatever comes our way.

Stoicism, as you might guess with the reference to Marcus Aurelius, was born in ancient Greece. The term Stoic comes from the Greek word *stoa poikile*, or painted porch, which refers to the public space in Athens where teachers and students regularly met and pontificated on life. The stoa was, in many ways, the center of Greek life. In the midst of this intellectual outburst, sometime around 300 BC, the man now considered the father of Stoicism first made a name for himself.

This was Zeno. Zeno's philosophy can be described simply enough: happiness comes as a result of living in accordance with nature's flow.

From Zeno's origination of Stoicism, the next notable Stoic was Epictetus, who is credited with the wisdom behind *The Enchiridion*, a handbook of thoughts on Stoicism. It begins in a compelling manner: "Some things are in our control and others not." Accepting that truth launches you on the way to being a Stoic.

Epictetus is where things really started to take on the modern form we know today. He went on to state, "There is only one way to happiness and that is to cease worrying about things which are beyond the power of our will."

Among the most fundamental tenets of Stoicism is the idea that we should attempt to control our lives. Investing emotional energy into things we cannot change or control, similar to Buddhism's avoidance of attachment, is what causes unhappiness, not the actual negative event or outcome itself.

He believed that focusing on things you *can* influence—your actions, responses, words, thoughts, and emotions (eventually)—were the real keys to happiness and fulfillment. We cannot change what happens to us, but we can change how we view them.

Epictetus spent his childhood as a Roman slave, and he lived most of his life on essentially one leg. He may have had a unique view on what it was to persevere and weather the storm of misfortune and still come out with a bright view of life.

Along the way in Stoic history, we also meet Seneca, whose personal letters remain instructive to this day. Finally, we shift to Marcus Aurelius, the renowned philosopher king himself.

This is his life philosophy in a nutshell:

> Everything that happens is either endurable or not. If it's endurable, then endure it. Stop complaining. If it's unendurable... then stop

complaining. Your destruction will mean its end as well. Just remember: you can endure anything your mind can make endurable, by treating it as in your interest to do so. In your interest, or in your nature.

Aurelius saw life as a giant neutral. Events will occur, happy and sad, but in reality, all events become how we choose to feel about them. Emotions, which ultimately determine our mood and satisfaction, come entirely from within and are a matter of our choosing. We only suffer as much as we allow ourselves to.

Accepting all of the above, much of Stoic philosophy then is about how to train ourselves to detach from our negative emotions and deal with the uncertainty of a lack of control. This is mentioned in the first of the three Stoic disciplines.

The Three Stoic Disciplines

The principles upon which Stoicism was founded have shifted dramatically due to different schools of thought and a gap of centuries between the most prominent practitioners and the founder, Zeno. Originally, Stoicism placed emphasis on the principles of ethics, physics, and logic.

But today's understanding of Stoicism focuses more on Epictetus's three principles.

1. "The Discipline of Desire," which has to do with *acceptance* of our fate.
2. "The Discipline of Action," which has to do with *philanthropy* or love of mankind.
3. "The Discipline of Assent," which has to do with *mindfulness* of our judgments.

Marcus Aurelius was taught by philosophers who possibly studied with Epictetus, although he never met him himself. One of the emperor's teachers introduced him to Epictetus's writings, and from that point, he was powerfully influenced by Epictetus. He also makes extensive mention of the Three Disciplines, which are important to understanding what informs his own writings.

1. The Discipline of Desire

This entails having an attitude of acceptance toward what comes our way. In a sense, it is similar to fatalism and being resigned to the gates. What happens is necessary for your growth and will help you in the long run.

Today we call the goal of this discipline *amor fati* or the loving acceptance of one's fate. This discipline is summed up in a passage from *The Enchiridion*: "Seek not for events to happen as you wish but wish events to happen as they do and your life will go smoothly and serenely."

But Stoics are not passive doormats with no ambitions and who allow life to happen to them. They simply accept what comes and think ahead to the next step in the best way possible.

For instance, Marcus Aurelius, despite a devastating plague and countless misfortunes beyond his control, led his weakened army repeatedly into battle to defend Rome against invading barbarian hordes. He prevailed despite the many obstacles to victory. If he'd failed, Rome would have been destroyed. As we'll see, the discipline of action explains this strange paradox: how can the Stoics combine acceptance with such famous endurance and courageous action?

In *amor fati*, you must embrace everything that has happened to you, as well as what will happen in the future. All events leading up to this moment were necessary precursors to the exact world you're standing in.

Suppose something happened we wish had not. Which is easier to change: our opinion and level of emotional impact or the event itself? The answer is obvious. The event lies in the past and cannot be changed. No matter how much you prepared, it still happened. But the way you view it can easily change. We do this by embracing *amor fati*. Stop fighting what reality is rather than resisting based on fantasy (that which did not happen). That's what happens when we can only (and sometimes even barely) control our actions in a volatile and unpredictable world.

The Stoics used the metaphor of a dog leashed to a moving cart. The dog can walk along with the cart despite having no control and still enjoy his walk and surroundings, or he can resist the cart with all of his might and be dragged for miles. It's our choice every single day whether we choose to be the dog that accepts his fate or be dragged. If we are dragged, we end up in the same destination, but have a dramatically poorer experience. If we can simply walk with the cart, we will be able to find the positive in that path.

2. The Discipline of Action

The discipline of action is living in harmony with the community of all mankind, which means benevolently wishing all of mankind to flourish and achieve happiness. No matter how malicious or deceptive they may be toward you, you must turn the other cheek, remain unaffected, and wish them well.

We cannot control others, but we are always in control of our own actions and responses. We always have the choice to act virtuously to help others reach happiness. It is similar to *amor fati* because our most frequent sources of unhappiness and tension will most likely be other people, yet we have to embrace their actions and words.

If someone is angry, we do not need to react in kind with anger or feel offended. We can choose to accept their anger, let it not impact us, and be reminded that it is meant to be instructive to our own happiness.

In other words, Stoics do their best to act with virtue while accepting the actions of others in a somewhat detached manner, whether pleasant or not. We should not let mere words hold such power over us.

3. The Discipline of Assent

The discipline of assent involves paying attention to our inner workings. We must be mindful enough to know what we are thinking—this is key to controlling your thoughts and emotions. There must be a measure of objectivity, otherwise you are lying to yourself and being overly impacted by your emotions.

Stoics are primarily interested in monitoring their judgments of *good* and *bad*. These simple judgments have the ability to influence our entire worldview. We may realize that we are viewing external events and the actions of people as negative or bad—but this is to ignore the fact that they are negative purely because we label them as such. This is unnecessary. Recall that emotions are a purely internal creation. The discipline of assent is the practice of catching yourself in this act of creating negative narratives around your life and quite literally changing your worldview.

In fact, nothing needs to be bad, negative, or unfortunate. This is a choice of judgment and labeling. Not everything needs to be transformed into a positive that makes you sing, yet certainly nothing needs to have the power to ruin your day.

So what do we get when we combine these three Stoic disciplines of acceptance, philanthropy, and mindfulness? We create a life philosophy that preaches introspection and self-awareness to remain calm and rational no matter the circumstances, even to those who would seek to maliciously hurt you. Focus only on what you can control (your emotions and actions), and let everything else play out as it will. This is a recipe for moving through life by rolling with the punches and coming back even stronger.

Turning the Obstacle Upside Down

"If you are pained by any external thing, it is not this thing that disturbs you, but your own judgment about it. And it is in your power to wipe out this judgment now."
– Marcus Aurelius

Key to Stoicism is plain and simple perception. Consider that two people can view a horrific car accident in different ways. One person can see it as a chance for a new car, while the other might only focus on the damage itself and assignment of guilt.

Perception is how we decide what events mean to us. Our perceptions can be like a lead ball chained to our feet, holding us back and making us weak, or they can be a great source of strength like a magical elixir.

How we see the world around us and how we interpret what happens to us makes a massive difference in how we get to live our lives. What we already learned from the Stoics is that they see external events not as good or bad but as indifferent. So it's not these events, because they are ultimately indifferent, but your own judgment of these events that matters.

This makes you responsible for your life. You don't control external events, but you control how you choose to look at them and then respond to them. And in the end, that's all that matters. As the famous Stoic turn of phrase says, you can *turn an obstacle upside down*. This means to look at even a negative occurrence as something that will ultimately benefit you later on or as a learning moment.

We are disturbed or delighted not by events but only by our judgment and perception of those events. What the Stoics tried to do was not get carried away by their initial impression about external events.

Something happens and we automatically get an impression about it. We can't do much about that. This is our emotional reaction, but it does not have to be our overall response.

So look at what happens objectively and dispassionately—it might be raining. And then choose your best reaction. The world won't end, and the activities you had planned for outdoors can be done another day. How might the rain force you to get creative or explore other untapped potential? What are the alternate perspectives you can adopt, rather than one of sadness or frustration? These alternate perspectives always exist, and you should train your ability to see them.

The truth is that you always have the ability to respond in a way that amounts to rolling with the punches. How might this obstacle become an opportunity, if only an opportunity to practice your sense of resiliency and patience?

Training Non-Reaction

It's not so simple as flipping a switch to turn the obstacle upside down and realize that your emotions are coming from entirely within you and under your control.

To be frank, most of our lives are too cushioned and comfortable for that to ever occur naturally. We have too many expectations and entitlements, and some of them are even justified. So what then?

The Stoics argued that if all we know is comfort, then we would be fragile and brittle when forced to inevitably experience pain or discomfort. By periodically practicing discomfort, we adapt and become stronger for those situations. We are able to understand that pain and discomfort are not things to be feared so much. This makes us emotionally more even-keeled.

Growth only occurs to those who are able to mentally and physically withstand discomfort. Stoicism might be the first philosophy to preach the maxim of "no pain, no gain."

Stoics were not masochist or anti-pleasure. They still enjoyed the fruits of life, but they recognized that proper perspective is needed to be non-reactive and also appreciate the good things.

Seneca puts it best:

> Set aside a certain number of days, during which you shall be content

with the scantiest and cheapest fare, with coarse and rough dress, saying to yourself the while: "Is this the condition that I feared?" It is precisely in times of immunity from care that the soul should toughen itself beforehand for occasions of greater stress, and it is while Fortune is kind that it should fortify itself against her violence. In days of peace the soldier performs maneuvers, throws up earthworks with no enemy in sight, and wearies himself by gratuitous toil, in order that he may be equal to unavoidable toil. If you would not have a man flinch when the crisis comes, train him before it comes.

To have a chance of keeping it together in the face of adversity, you must practice. Toughen up before you need to, and you'll be prepared for anything.

Seneca suggested living as a pauper for a period of time. Wear old, unflattering clothes, eat sparsely and only plain food, and even attempt to sleep on the floor. There are various degrees to try this. You can go for a week with only simple food such as bread and soup. You can spend a month on a tight daily budget. Maybe you want to drink only water for a couple of days.

Training your discomfort muscle makes you view hardship in a different light. *Been there, done that, what's the big deal?* This allows you to detach from the circumstances and move on more quickly. You'll gain the confidence in yourself that you can handle adversity and also appreciate what you have in a powerful way. These perspectives make it difficult to overly react to negative situations.

Seneca reminds us, "It is precisely in times of immunity from care that the soul should toughen itself beforehand for occasions of greater stress... If you would not have a man flinch when the crisis comes, train him before it comes."

Instead of putting yourself in uncomfortable situations, you can also purposefully say *no* to pleasurable situations.

None of this makes life harder; in fact, it makes it easier. By undertaking acts of discomfort, you harden yourself against future misfortunes. If you only know comfort, then you might be traumatized when you are forced to experience pain or any other sort of discomfort in the future, as you surely will eventually. Optimally, you'll be immune to discomfort.

Take away some comfort from your life and it'll remind you of how comfortable and happy your life actually is. By purposefully forgoing some of our pleasures and comforts, we can create a greater sense of gratitude. Voluntary discomfort lets us enjoy more of what we already have. And maybe it takes away some of our cravings for more.

Another way of training your non-reactivity and sense of gratitude is to practice negative visualization.

Stoics recommended to periodically spend time imagining that we have lost the things we value most. Imagine you have lost your family, your health, or your job—whatever you place a high value upon. Deliberately reflect on each value as if it has disappeared. Think about what you would be missing and how that would impact your daily life. Think about the despair you would feel.

Negative visualization is a powerful counter to human desire. Suddenly, you will be forced to realize that you already have what makes you happy beyond measure. You will realize and appreciate what you have in your life, and you will also find that the desire for more has completely halted.

When you spend time deliberately realizing that everything you love and cherish could be taken from you tomorrow by some sick twist of fate, *you feel humbled.* You realize how many gifts and blessings you truly have. You see the real worth of everything surrounding you. This is a difficult state of mind in which to be consumed with desire and worry.

Focusing on What You Can Control

Remember the first line of Epictetus's *Enchiridion*? "Make the best use of what is in your power, and take the rest as it happens. Some things are up to us and some things are not up to us."

This is deemed the Stoic circle of control. We must carefully distinguish between what is within our own power and what is not. Up to us are our voluntary choices, namely our actions and judgments, while *everything else* is not under our control. This means that right off the bat, you must accept that you have no control over 90% of your worries and concerns. No matter what you do or how virtuous you are, you cannot affect the outcome. So why keep your concerns dangling in your mind?

We only control our own actions and thoughts, and we have no choice but to accept the outcome. From our end, we can ensure that we are doing our best and putting our entire effort into something. But if we have done everything within our power, that's where our control really ends.

The things that are up to you, your thoughts and your actions, are the most important things in life. The most appealing aspect of Stoicism is that we are responsible for our flourishing because all that truly matters in life is up to us.

So the key lesson to take away here is to focus our attention and efforts where we actually have control and then let the universe take care of the rest. This turns out to be a very small subset of actions and thoughts, which is comforting in itself. Where a to-do list was once 10 items, you will find that it can easily be shaved down to three items.

The Stoics used the archer analogy to explain what to stop wasting your time on.

An archer is trying to hit a target. He has done his best to prepare for this moment. He has practiced and trained, carefully selected his bow and arrow, and is in a state of intense mental focus. He can control each and every moment, right up until he looses the arrow. And then?

Whether or not he hits the target is not up to him. As the arrow takes flight, any number of things could happen, some predictable and some not. He could simply have not prepared very well and have poor aim. But a gust of wind could also disrupt the arrow's path, a bird could fly into the arrow's path, or the target itself could be jolted. Another person might also shoot the target first or sabotage the archer.

None of this reflects on the archer himself. He did his best and left the rest to the flow of nature. This is all we can ever do, so the outcomes we get should be equally accepted. *Amor fati.*

Epictetus went on to state,

So make a practice at once of saying to every strong impression: "An impression is all you are, not the source of the impression." Then test and assess it with your criteria, but one primarily: ask, "Is this something that is, or is not, in my control?" And if it's not one of the things that you control, be ready with the reaction, "Then it's none of my concern."

Check your impressions and ask yourself whether it's up to you or not. If it's up to you, then do something about it. If not, take it as it is. It was already written in stone before you got there, and it will be written in stone after you leave. Nothing you could have done would make a difference. Picture someone who prefers chocolate ice cream but you serve them vanilla ice cream—you may have slaved over the vanilla ice cream, but that simply doesn't matter. It was never up to you, despite your efforts and planning. There is nothing left to do but move forward.

Think of your day and think of the things you have complete control of, things you have some control of, and the things you have no control of. You should eventually come to the realization that the only thing you have complete control of is yourself. The only thing we control entirely is our self, our will, and our intentions.

You can't control if the sun will come out tomorrow; you can plan for it, but why worry about it? Focus on your own actions and improve them as you can; give yourself the best opportunity for success and the outcome you want. But in the end, a hurricane could come and destroy everything. So why worry?

Stoicism is a life philosophy that anticipates hardships. When good things happen to us, it's easy to feel strong and resilient. But it's only when we face hardship that we shape the narrative of our lives. Just like our emotions, the way we view our lives comes exclusively from us internally and doesn't really have any correlation with the reality that we live in.

Takeaways:

- Stoicism has been around in many forms, but the most widespread and modern version comes from Marcus Aurelius, the famous philosopher king of the Roman Empire. It is a direct philosophy on how to live better and remain more fulfilled in the face of a harsh world full of suffering.
- Stoicism is driven by three main disciplines: the discipline of desire (your unhappiness stems from your desires and unwillingness to accept other outcomes), action (act toward others regardless of how they do to you), and assent (be mindful of your thoughts and actions, as they are entirely within your control and in fact manmade).
- So what do we get when we combine these three Stoic disciplines of acceptance, philanthropy, and mindfulness? We create a life philosophy that preaches introspection and self-awareness to remain calm and rational no matter the circumstances, even to those who would seek to maliciously

hurt you. Focus only on what you can control (your emotions and actions), and let everything else play out as it will.

- You must learn to turn the obstacle upside down. This means our happiness depends on our perception and judgment of external events. In fact, all events are neutral, and we only assign them value due to our perceptions. We actively prevent ourselves from turning the obstacle upside down and viewing hardships through a more positive lens. If tragedy happens, life must move on. This is entirely up to you.

- Turning the obstacle upside down is not easy. Controlling your emotions and responding rather than reacting is the focus of many philosophies. Stoicism takes a different view on how to train this type of non-reactiveness. We must induce voluntary discomfort and also practice negative visualization. This dramatically changes our expectations and sense of gratitude and allows us to become more resilient in our thoughts.

- Finally, Stoicism encourages you to focus only on what is within your control and accept that which is not. You can control your efforts and actions but almost never the outcomes. This is life. One path leads you to happiness, while the other leads you to perpetual dissatisfaction. Again, this choice is entirely upon your shoulders.

Chapter 7. Taoism and the Action of Nonaction

Most people are unfamiliar with Taoism and probably mix it up with Daoism, Buddhism, or Confucianism. Taoism and Daoism actually refer to the same belief system, while Confucianism and Buddhism are entirely distinct, as you have read in this book.

It's almost understandable because most philosophy tends to focus on Western schools of thought, and the origins of Taoism are somewhat unclear. But where Buddhism preaches the Eightfold Path and Confucianism emphasizes the value of investing in your relationships, Taoism actually has the most in common with

Stoicism. They are the ultimate philosophies that preach how to roll with the punches and make the best of a bad situation.

Taoism was prominent starting from the Tang Dynasty of China, so much so that the emperor Xuanzong made it a state religion. Even though it was originally rooted in pagan practices, today there is no real central deity besides the Tao itself, which is a rather ambiguous concept.

What we think we know is that it all started from *Lao-Tzu*, who lived in the sixth century BC. Legend has it that Lao-Tzu had no father, was conceived when a shooting star passed by, and came out of his mother's womb at age 82.

A famous historian tells a somewhat more believable account of how Lao-Tzu came to be so wise and learned. It seems that he used to work in the Chinese government but soon grew disillusioned with the corruption he saw and decided to exile himself rather than participate in it. As Lao-

Tzu was journeying west and leaving China, he was asked to write a book on his beliefs of how government and people in general could improve, and this ended up becoming the *Tao Te Ching* (roughly translated into *The Book of the Way*). After this, he was never seen again. You could say he went out on a high note.

The *Tao Te Ching* is not actually a type of holy text or scripture in the conventional sense. It's more of a how-to book for achieving fulfillment, balance, and even on how to run government effectively. It talks about the Tao and how important it is to seeking happiness and inner peace. And this is all expressed through poetry.

Sadly, the *Tao Te Ching* was most likely not written by Lao-Tzu before he vanished into vapor, and it's possible that he may not have existed at all. But the origins aren't particularly important as much as the significance of its message. The *Tao Te Ching* prescribes that peace and fulfillment are much easier to find than you might think; they happen naturally if you live with the Tao and don't fight it.

Taoism is *all* about living in accordance with the Tao. So what is the Tao and how can we add this to our library of life philosophies?

The Tao of It All

For most, the very definition of Taoism is confusing. That's probably because the Tao is by definition indefinable. It is subjective and different to everyone—a stark contrast from other belief systems and philosophies that have very concrete goals to aim for. For instance, Aristotle and Confucius provide exact virtues to try to embody, and these are the same for everyone. The Tao documents the individual journeys we all go through and how they are all interconnected.

The earliest Chinese character for Tao is formed by combining the characters for movement and leg. So the Tao is a picture of a person moving along a path. Thus, Tao is usually translated into English as "the way" or "the path." So far so good; each of us has a life path that is unique and different from that of others.

Here's what the *Tao Te Ching* says:

There was something undifferentiated and yet complete,
Which existed before Heaven and Earth.
Soundless and formless it depends on nothing and does not change.
It operates everywhere and is free from danger.
It may be considered the mother of the universe.
I do not know its name; I call it Tao.

This might seem like a preamble to actually describing the Tao, but that's just it—the Tao is not a thing, object, or substance in the conventional sense. It cannot be perceived, but it can be observed in the things of the world. Think of it as an omnipresent background force that connects all of us, with waves that ripple outward like when you drop a pebble into a lake. We are all floating in the same waters of life and the universe; waves, droughts, ripples, and even floods will occur, but we still flow onward. This natural cause and effect interconnection is the Tao.

Thus, to be a Taoist is to attempt to align yourself with the Tao, this natural flow of the world. Try your best, and accept and act on whatever comes. If the current of the river is pushing you one way, don't resist it; swim with it and make the best of it, even if it is against your initial expectations.

If we live within this flow and honor it, we will be happier and more peaceful. All too often, we are living in direct conflict with this type of natural flow. When man seeks his own plan rather than the eternal plan of the Tao, he invites ills, suffering, and evil. We create unhappiness and tension by resisting the flow. It doesn't only concern you; when everything and everyone is connected, you are disrupting the happiness and harmony of your surroundings if you resist the flow.

The flow governs everything. It governs the changing seasons, how a river carves through a mountain, and the passage of time. We all have our role in this flow and should accept it when it happens to us. Nature moves slowly, methodically, its underlying principles only observable to a certain degree. In this respect, understanding the Tao means letting go and submitting to nature's flow. We must listen and adapt and ultimately let go rather than try to force our own flow.

The most famous symbol of Taoism is the *yin-yang*. It is the visual embodiment of the duality of life and balance. For instance, day and night or male and female. There is constant change, but the balance always exists in a type of equilibrium and harmony. This is also the result of living in accordance with the Tao. Indeed, you might say that the yin-yang duality is what causes the natural flow of the Tao as we go from one extreme to the other. They can never exist in isolation from one another, and thus represents the only constant we will ever have: change itself.

You can probably imagine that the Tao is best reached through simplicity and rolling with the punches in life. What contributes to living within that natural flow? Finally, we get to the question of how to actually seek Tao in real life. That's by seeking *wu wei*. It's almost staggering in its simplicity.

Seeking *Wu Wei*

The concept of *wu wei* is typically translated as *the action of nonaction*.

This is the art of moving in unison with the natural flow of the Tao to achieve goals rather than crudely going against the grain. Its hallmarks are patience, timing, simplicity, spontaneity, attention, and moderation. This might seem like a passive way of living and that you won't accomplish many goals at all.

But if you possess that mindset, then you are pursuing your own path and not the natural, peaceful flow of the Tao. *Wu wei* puts you into alignment with the ebb and flow of life's flow. Go with the flow and make the best of what comes at you, and you will be sure to find happiness. Don't force things, but this doesn't mean that you can't make a real effort. It is clear that *wu wei* and the Tao are in direct opposition to your individual ego—when you can want for less, you are simply more grateful and humble.

It is suggested that humans ought to be like water for it is obedient and flexible, yet it always seems to overcome things with strength and resilience.

Act without action.
Pursue without interfering.
Taste the tasteless.
Make the small big and the few many.
Return animosity with virtue.
Meet the difficult while it is easy.
Meet the big while it is small.
The most difficult in the world
Must be easy in its beginning.
The biggest in the world
Is small in its beginning.
So, the sage never strives for greatness,
And can therefore accomplish greatness.
Lightly given promises

Must meet with little trust.
Taking things lightly
Must lead to big difficulties.
So, the sage regards things as difficult,
And thereby avoids difficulty.

Researcher Alan Watts uses the example of a boat. He explains that *rowing* is a thoughtless and inefficient way of moving a boat across the water. This is because it requires immense strain and hardship to move against the current of a body of water. On the other hand, *sailing* uses the forces of nature, namely the power of the wind, to skillfully move and maneuver the boat.

This is what *wu wei* means—recognizing the forces of nature and acting accordingly. The action we take is determined by the time, places, and forces that all come together at a unique moment in time. You can envision an outline and stages of progress for any action, but you may actually thwart bigger messages coming through if you push your agenda too much. Put your sails up and prepare them for action, but recognize that the wind will blow when it chooses to, not when you want it to.

The idea of nonaction is that instead of having the conscious will, intention, or demand that something happen deliberately, you have the inclination, willingness, or preference for that something to happen. The presupposition is that by not being attached to a specific end result, you can allow what is actually motivating and generating your actions— not your own personal agenda or ego—to occur and the larger purpose is therefore served.

This is achieved by freedom from our ego and the ideals that we have forced upon ourselves and onto others. Kindness, sincerity, and humility should be cultivated. Pride and glory are to be avoided. Education, wealth, power, and even family ties are impediments to following the natural flow. Desire and wanting will feel futile and hopeless and cause pain; flowing with the moment is calming and easy.

The way of the Tao is in accordance with nature while resistance to the Tao is unnatural and causes friction. The best way for a person to live, according to Taoism, is to submit to whatever life brings and be flexible. If a person adapts to the changes in life easily, that person will be happy; if a person resists the changes in life, that person will be unhappy. One's ultimate goal is to live at peace with the way of the Tao and recognize that everything that happens in life should be accepted as part of the eternal force that binds and moves through all things.

The doctrine of nonaction requires an immense amount of courage because you have to give up a sense of control. You have to be able to admit that you do not know. You also have to be able to identify when you're operating in essentially an emotional, mental, or psychic state of nonaction.

Wu wei can be applied to all aspects of our everyday life. When you feel inspired and motivated, take advantage and work with great vigor and determination. But you have to accept that eventually you are going to burn out because you can only paddle against the current for so long. You have to know when effort is useful and when it is wasted. Embrace the fall and do not resist it. Remember, you're not doing nothing— you're taking action through nonaction. Set yourself up for success, and the rest takes care of itself.

Taoism is about acceptance and gratitude, plain and simple. When you can accept your life and feel gratitude, then it is nearly impossible to have expectations or feel disappointment. In this way, Taoism shares quite a few similarities with Buddhism and Stoicism—Buddhism is about releasing all attachments, where Stoicism is about acknowledging and growing from discomfort. Together, these philosophies create an incredibly resilient mind.

The Butterfly Dream

One of the most famous parables, or thought experiments, in philosophy also stems from Taoism. It comes from the Chinese philosopher Zhuangzi, who is generally considered the second-most important figure after Lao-Tzu. He asserted that one day he fell asleep and dreamed that he was a butterfly.

> Once upon a time, I, Zhuangzi, dreamt I was a butterfly, fluttering hither and thither, to all intents and purposes a butterfly. I was conscious only of my happiness as a butterfly, unaware that I was Zhuangzi. Soon I awakened, and there I was, veritably myself again. Now I do not know whether I was then a man dreaming I was a butterfly, or whether I am now a butterfly, dreaming I am a man. Between a man and a butterfly there is necessarily a distinction. The transition is called the transformation of material things.

When he woke up, he did not know whether he really was a man who had dreamed he was a butterfly or whether he was a butterfly now dreaming he was a man. Was it such a realistic dream that he couldn't tell the difference, or was there a deeper message?

Probably the latter. There are many interpretations of this parable, but my personal interpretation is that it represents the importance of the natural universal flow. The butterfly dream is the ultimate example of living in accordance with the Tao and riding *wu wei*.

What we believe simply may not be true. In fact, our senses and reasoning may be deceiving us. But that doesn't matter, and it takes us out of the Tao when we struggle to live up to an expectation of whatever being we are.

Struggling to define our reality and whether or not he was a butterfly or a man fits neatly with the concept of going with the flow of *wu wei*. If Zhuangzi were to simply embrace *wu wei*, would it matter which organism he is? No, he would paddle with the current and keep on flowing.

Remember, it is when we desire things that go against the natural flow of the Tao that we grow disappointed. To Zhuangzi, it simply did not matter if he was a man or butterfly in the end—he would continue to seek the natural flow. But if he had a desire, then he would be consumed with doubt and grow unhappy.

Takeaways:

- Taoism is often mistaken for something else, but that's only based on cursory knowledge. In fact, Taoism is incredibly distinct from other belief systems and philosophies. First and foremost, of course, is because the Tao is an undefined cosmic force that compels us to go with the flow and desire less. This stands in stark contrast to other belief systems.
- The Tao is the natural flow of our life and world, and we should seek to find it, for it is what will create the most fulfillment and peace. Just as importantly, we should ensure that we do not resist it and can live in harmony

174

with it. This concept is embodied in *wu wei*, which describes how to seek the Tao in concrete terms.

- *Wu wei* is translated as the action of nonaction, and it is the ultimate embodiment of the flow of the Tao. We are all paddling boats in an ocean, and we can either choose to paddle against the current or with it. Paddle with it. Take action when the natural flow of life allows you to and adapt to the current when it inevitably changes. Accept these outcomes and release the expectations you might have.
- Zhuangzi's butterfly dream is the epitome of seeking the flow of the Tao. In fact, it doesn't even matter if he is a man or butterfly in the end—he will cast aside his expectations and desires and continue with whatever path he sees available.

Cheat Sheet

Chapter 1. What's Your Philosophy?

- Philosophy means different things to different people, so I would like to present what it means to me. It's about self-understanding and then taking and stealing from some of history's greatest thinkers to form the basis of what makes you happy. It's only when you understand yourself that you can move forward in a way that is more likely to lead to your happiness. In other words, clearer thinking leads to self-understanding, which leads to your life philosophy emerging. Formulating your own life philosophy is key to the life you want, and it influences all of your daily actions, big and small.
- The trolley dilemma is a demonstration of the other major benefit of delving into philosophical thought. You learn how to

think. You learn how to argue, debate, and reason. You learn how a seemingly innocent or simple question can have wide-ranging implications and consequences. You can learn to thrive in the ungrounded, abstract, and ambiguous. And when you direct this thinking toward deeper questions that philosophy presents, you can begin to understand yourself more than ever before. Philosophy won't directly feed your family or put a roof over your head, but indirectly, it leads to all that and more.

Chapter 2. Aristotle, Living Virtuously, and the Golden Mean

- We can consider this chapter to be the life philosophy of Aristotle with regards to seeking happiness and fulfillment or, in his term, eudaemonia. It was all about virtue for him. Eudaemonia sprung from living a virtuous life, and virtue was attained by adhering to the Golden Mean.
- The Golden Mean is a set of 11 traits to exemplify and ensure that you are not

using them to excess or deficiency. In other words, it's just as you would assume from the title: a life of moderation and even keel. Yes, too much of a good thing ends up being a bad thing; there are always tradeoffs. When you live within these 11 traits, you will automatically be living the life that makes you fulfilled, no matter the outcomes or circumstances. Of note, you must intentionally (and not accidentally) be embodying these traits to be virtuous.

- The Golden Mean is a means of finding eudaemonia internally from your own actions. Aristotle also addressed how to externally find fulfillment—through the right types of friendships. He articulated three types: pleasure-based, utility-based, and virtue-based. Of course, he's all about virtues again here and the mutual growth and respect they encourage.

Chapter 3. Buddhism and the Elimination of Attachment

- Our conventional view of Buddhism is that it's about giving up all of your material possessions and joining a monastery. While misguided, this speaks to the central tenet of Buddhism: ceasing attachments.
- Buddhism as a life philosophy is quite instructive because it lays out a premise, a problem, and a clear solution to the problem. The premise is the Three Marks of Existence, which describe the realities of human beings: everything is impermanent, life is suffering, and who you are changes from moment to moment.
- The problem is the Four Noble Truths, which stem from the Three Marks of Existence, which describe why humans are unhappy as well as the key to overcoming it. They are: life is suffering, suffering comes from attachment, letting go of attachment ends suffering, and the Eightfold Path is the way to happiness.
- The solution is the Eightfold Path, which is a series of eight large and small actions to perform to achieve enlightenment and freedom from

attachment. They must be embodied, not simply ruminated over. The purpose is to create a sense of enlightenment and freedom from attachment by living the right way. They are: right understanding, right intentions, right speech, right action, right livelihood, right effort, right mindfulness, and right concentration.

Chapter 4. Descartes and Seeking Absolute Truth

- Rene Descartes helps us live a better life through embracing doubt and seeking to discover only the absolute truth. He upended centuries of philosophical and scientific thought with this simple notion. His thoughts on the matter came to a head in his book *Meditations on First Philosophy*, which contains six meditations. The first three are more relevant to our purposes of finding truth and gaining certainty that our belief *is* the truth. The first three meditations are part of a process of finding what is true.

- Meditation 1 is about knowing that our beliefs are potentially flawed in two main ways: our sensations can lie to us, and our reasoning can be incorrect. Descartes poked holes in just about everything we know using the dream problem and the demon problem. The dream problem supposes that since our senses are the same when we dream, we cannot rely on them to tell the truth. The demon problem supposes that a demon could be feeding us our reasoning, and thus we can't be sure that it is the truth. So once we understand that much of what we think is not necessarily true, we move onto the next step.
- Meditation 2 is about finding beliefs that are absolutely true, and for this, Descartes turns to one of the most famous thought experiments: *cogito ergo sum*. This of course means "I think; therefore, I am." Despite demons or dreams, because Descartes has made a thought, it means he exists. This was his process of finding an absolute truth through logic. It was the most basic starting place to build from.

- Meditation 3 follows on Meditation 2's assertion of truth. From *cogito ergo sum*, Descartes suggests the standard for truth is that which is *clear and distinct*. This is a relatively hazy definition, and he makes it clear later on that he considers the word of God to be clear and distinct. Remember, one of his main goals for doubt was to gain greater confidence in the existence of God. But don't let his methods of doubt for finding truth be obscured by this last step.
- Understand that which can be false (most beliefs). Second, find a method for proving the truth of a matter. This is a mindset that can be applied to nearly every aspect of your life; it can ensure that you aren't being suckered or laboring under falsehoods. When you are sure about what you know, then your actions can follow your intentions.

Chapter 5. Confucius and the Five Relationships

- Confucianism, despite the intention, has been an integral part of Chinese and East Asian culture for centuries. Although Confucius was not necessarily greatly celebrated in his own lifetime, his teachings became official state doctrine hundreds of years after his death. It starts with the premise that the harmony of society is more important than almost any individual need, and everything else springs out of that. It may seem counterintuitive that a philosophy so focused on others can bring us happiness, but it simply reminds us of our roles and adjusts our expectations.
- The main aspect of Confucianism as it pertains to a life philosophy is the emphasis on the five relationships. Confucius believed that our adherence to specific roles in specific relationships created a harmonious society and made our place within it harmonious and happy as well. It is noteworthy that three of the relationships relate to immediate family. The five relationships are ruler and subject, father and son,

elder brother and younger brother, husband and wife, and friend and friend. The first four relationships all have a power dynamic, and as a result, deference is expected.

- The other aspect of Confucianism is the five Confucian virtues. They speak to self-restraint and propriety, righteousness, honesty, love of your fellow man, and wisdom and character. These ultimately have the same impact as Aristotle's virtues—a good blueprint or code of behavior to shoot for. Act accordingly and you will only be rewarded.

Chapter 6. Marcus Aurelius and Embracing Discomfort

- Stoicism has been around in many forms, but the most widespread and modern version comes from Marcus Aurelius, the famous philosopher king of the Roman Empire. It is a direct philosophy on how to live better and remain more fulfilled in the face of a harsh world full of suffering.

- Stoicism is driven by three main disciplines: the discipline of desire (your unhappiness stems from your desires and unwillingness to accept other outcomes), action (act toward others regardless of how they do to you), and assent (be mindful of your thoughts and actions, as they are entirely within your control and in fact manmade).
- So what do we get when we combine these three Stoic disciplines of acceptance, philanthropy, and mindfulness? We create a life philosophy that preaches introspection and self-awareness to remain calm and rational no matter the circumstances, even to those who would seek to maliciously hurt you. Focus only on what you can control (your emotions and actions), and let everything else play out as it will.
- You must learn to turn the obstacle upside down. This means our happiness depends on our perception and judgment of external events. In fact, all events are neutral, and we only assign them value due to our perceptions. We actively prevent ourselves from turning

the obstacle upside down and viewing hardships through a more positive lens. If tragedy happens, life must move on. This is entirely up to you.

- Turning the obstacle upside down is not easy. Controlling your emotions and responding rather than reacting is the focus of many philosophies. Stoicism takes a different view on how to train this type of non-reactiveness. We must induce voluntary discomfort and also practice negative visualization. This dramatically changes our expectations and sense of gratitude and allows us to become more resilient in our thoughts.

- Finally, Stoicism encourages you to focus only on what is within your control and accept that which is not. You can control your efforts and actions but almost never the outcomes. This is life. One path leads you to happiness, while the other leads you to perpetual dissatisfaction. Again, this choice is entirely upon your shoulders.

Chapter 7. Taoism and the Action of Nonaction

- Taoism is often mistaken for something else, but that's only based on cursory knowledge. In fact, Taoism is incredibly distinct from other belief systems and philosophies. First and foremost, of course, is because the Tao is an undefined cosmic force that compels us to go with the flow and desire less. This stands in stark contrast to other belief systems.

- The Tao is the natural flow of our life and world, and we should seek to find it, for it is what will create the most fulfillment and peace. Just as importantly, we should ensure that we do not resist it and can live in harmony with it. This concept is embodied in *wu wei*, which describes how to seek the Tao in concrete terms.

- *Wu wei* is translated as the action of nonaction, and it is the ultimate embodiment of the flow of the Tao. We are all paddling boats in an ocean, and we can either choose to paddle against the current or with it. Paddle with it. Take action when the natural flow of life allows you to and adapt to the current when it inevitably changes. Accept these outcomes and release the expectations you might have.

- Zhuangzi's butterfly dream is the epitome of seeking the flow of the Tao. In fact, it doesn't even matter if he is a man or butterfly in the end—he will cast aside his expectations and desires and continue with whatever path he sees available.

www.ingramcontent.com/pod-product-compliance
Lightning Source LLC
Chambersburg PA
CBHW070931030426
42336CB00014BA/2618